The development of independent reading
Reading support explained

Peter Guppy and
Margaret Hughes

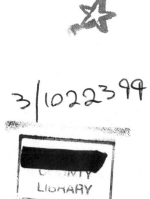

Open
Bucki

To Janet and John

Ronnie
and
Anne

Open University Press
Celtic Court
22 Ballmoor
Buckingham
MK18 1XW

email: enquiries@openup.co.uk
world wide web: http://www.openup.co.uk

and
325 Chestnut Street
Philadelphia, PA 19106, USA

First Published 1999

A catalogue record of this book is available from the British Library

ISBN   0 335 20152 0 (pb)

Library of Congress Cataloging-in-Publication Data
Guppy, Peter, 1944–
  The development of independent reading/Peter Guppy and Margaret Hughes.
      p.   cm.
  Includes bibliographical references and index.
  ISBN 0-335-20152-0 (pbk)
  1. Reading (Elementary)   2. Reading–Parent participation.   I. Hughes, Margaret.   II. Title.
LB1573.G94   1998
372.4—dc21   98-5420 CIP

Copy-edited by The Running H
Typeset by Type Study, Scarbor
Printed in Great Britain by Redv

Contents

List of figures

Introduction

This book is for people who are involved in the teaching of reading:

- practising teachers who want to know more;
- teachers new to the classroom;
- teachers new to teaching reading;
- postholders (language/literacy and special educational needs) who inform others, including parents;
- lecturers in initial teacher training, and their students.

It has arisen out of our work as reading teachers. Working alongside class teachers, helpers and parents, we have been made routinely aware of an enduring current of interest in reading in general and, in particular, how best to help children learn to read.

The questions we meet in schools show a continuing need to extend and update knowledge of major issues of reading. They come from various quarters, and often betray a degree of real urgency. A typical week of travelling round schools can produce a crop of questions of which the following are representative:

TEACHER: 'I've taught Year 3 for years, but this year I've got Year 6. Can you explain the differences?'

This teacher is in effect asking for an overview, which would show the relevance of her familiar practice in relation to the continuum of reading development. She will be reassured by the recognition that, because there are certain permanent components of reading, the elements important for Year 3 reading will be just as important for Year 6. Only the approaches and emphases will differ.

PARENT: 'What do *you* actually do when you hear a child read?'

Here, a parent is exploring how to tailor reading support to a child's stage of development, an art often misrepresented under the one umbrella of 'Hearing reading'. He needs explanations about the considerably different types of support required by his two sons, one aged 5, one almost 9.

CLASSROOM ASSISTANT: 'Have you any ideas for helping children to work out the hard words for themselves?'

The classroom assistant, having spent many hours 'Hearing reading', is now asking in fact for further knowledge of cues, those providers of the information which a reader uses to solve a problem word.

LANGUAGE/LITERACY POSTHOLDER: 'That phonological awareness course was fascinating stuff. I'm talking about it at next week's staff meeting. How can I make it user-friendly, at the same time showing where it fits in?'

The Language/literacy postholder is aware of her responsibility to present new knowledge mapped onto a coherent picture of the reading process, and with such relevance that it is used, used properly and in its rightful place.

As we travel from school to school we see this strong current of interest in reading remain constant, despite the impact in recent years of one initiative after another. This is evidence of a professionalism which is to be applauded. However, schools have been bombarded by changes which have not been accompanied by the support those changes deserved. For instance:

- Successive versions of the National Curriculum, which initially had the paradoxical effect of actually reducing the time available for reading, prescribe the standards children should reach.
    But there is a need for descriptions of how children are to reach them. The National Curriculum is an inventory. There is also a need for manuals.
- Ofsted inspections promote the re-examination of reading provision, both before the inspection, and afterwards in the action plans.
    Schools need to be able to refer to detailed descriptions of practice, based on clear accounts of good theory, when replanning their reading policies.
- Appraisal schemes are widely in place, one of the positive outcomes of which should be training. Yet even as this need for refresher courses has grown, so opportunities have waned. There is less money for training, and furthermore, the number of actual sources of training has diminished.
    Schools need support in delivering their own training.
- Alongside all that is happening in schools, there is also a huge increase in public debate about reading – led by government requirements, daily discussed in the media, reflected in parents' anxieties.
    A more widely promoted understanding is needed, of what 'the basics' really are, to dispel lingering myths of a traditional golden age.

- Colleges and universities also are under pressure to produce newly qualified teachers ready to go out into schools fully competent to teach children to read. As the prospect of responsibility for real flesh-and-blood children draws near, what final-year student does not feel anxious about having sufficient detailed knowledge of this task?

  Clearly, training should not come to an abrupt end at the point of qualifying.
- And finally, what of the initiatives ahead? Even as we write we await the effects of 1998 as the Year of Reading, and especially the impact of the Literacy Hour. The swiftness of its inception for some will come as a shock, for some as a threat, for all as a new demand on expertise.

  Many teachers will be looking to strengthen their knowledge base, and to complement it with a bank of practical ideas.

These are some of the concerns, then, with which we are routinely presented. But our travelling around schools involves us in far more than just listening to teachers' concerns. We respond, in practical ways. An advantage of our role is that as well as working with groups we can also work with children one-to-one. The insights into the development of independent reading we gain from such close observation we are then able to pass on to teachers. These insights, and the overall picture they provide, form the basis of our in-service work, and help us in planning and presenting parents' meetings. We have based our book upon this work.

So, within the pages of this book there are episodes of teaching (the written equivalent of video clips), in which we look over the adult's shoulder to observe two things:

- significant reading-events as they happen;
- how the adult uses these to further the child's development.

These are accompanied by:

- a description of the continuum of reading development;
- information on the role of cues;
- explicit teaching advice;
- sample 'scripts' to help the teacher translate theoretical suggestions into a classroom voice;
- ready-made materials for passing on this information in in-service and other training, i.e. photocopiable masters for OHP transparencies, information sheets, and, as focus for discussion, tables of pros and cons on various reading issues;
- adaptable outlines for activities at parents' meetings.

Five stages of reading development are described, named not numbered, to reflect the gradual changes in support to meet the different needs of each stage: Bookbinding, Chiming in, Cue talk, Assisted reading, Branching out.

Chapters 1 to 5 cover one stage each. These are prefaced by a Rationale outlining the reading process and including an observation sheet ready for practical use (the Positive Cueing Observation Sheet, Figure R.7).

Finally, Chapter 6 deals with the training of parents and helpers, and discusses the concept that they, with the teachers, constitute a team. These seven chapters can be the framework for a course.

But we also intend it to be a readable reference book, for reading first almost recreationally, to gain a concept of the reading continuum, and thereafter referred to as needed.

However, the ideas in the book do not stem solely from our own observations. We are also influenced by significant voices from the worlds of education and research. Not only do these fuel our own interest and shape our day-to-day work, but they also provide essential validity to what we have to say in talking to individual teachers and developing in-service training.

So next, by returning briefly to the four opening questions, we mention some of those who have influenced our thinking in the major areas of reading theory which form the key themes of the book.

Firstly, the teacher's question: 'I've taught Year 3 for years, but this year I've got Year 6. Can you explain the differences?'

This question requires that we identify the permanent components of reading. They are embodied in our basic model of reading, and we refer to them frequently throughout the book as Reading the lines, Reading Between the lines and Reading Beyond the lines. Gray (1960) previously identified and labelled these three components, but he presented them as a linear sequence of skills. From the essence of Gray's idea we have developed a view of the three components as:

- not necessarily operating in one fixed sequence;
- interdependent;
- all equally influential in providing the reader with information.

Secondly, the parent's question: 'What do *you* actually do when you hear a child read?'

To address this question we detail the ways in which one-to-one reading support must adapt to fit the child's stage of development. This is a perspective on learning drawn from Vygotsky (1978), and we are grateful to Wray (1995: 48) for the following succinct account:

> Vygotsky put forward the notion that children first experience a particular cognitive activity with expert practitioners. The child is first a spectator as the majority of the cognitive work is done by the expert (parent or teacher), then a novice as s/he starts to take over some of the work under the close supervision of the expert. As the child grows in experience and capability in performing the task, the expert passes over greater and greater responsibility but still acts as a guide, assisting the child at problematic points. Eventually the child assumes full responsibility for the task with the expert still present in the role of supportive audience.

Thirdly, the classroom assistant's query: 'Have you any ideas for helping children to work out the hard words for themselves?'

This question takes us to the use of cues, a concept central to reading. Goodman (1976a: 129) gave an early description of their crucial role: 'All reading behaviour is caused. It is cued or miscued.' He explained further: 'Readers select from graphophonic, syntactic and semantic cues . . .' (Goodman 1976b: 833). More recently, Adams (1990: 422) attests to their indispensability, pointing out: 'The text provides but one of the sources of information. The rest must come from the reader's own prior knowledge.' These two types of cue, which are identified by Goodman as within and without the text, and by Adams as two sources of information, are both present in our model, and termed by us 'Fine' and 'Broad'. We consider Fine and Broad to be of equal importance.

Furthermore, our model indicates a vital area where the two overlap. Such an integrating approach is endorsed by a wide circle of literacy professionals:

> There is now a body of rigorously controlled research which shows that the most effective training programmes are those which develop the child's ability to use both phonological and holistic processing, rather than programmes which emphasise one approach to the exclusion of the other.
>
> (Bradley 1990: 98)

In coining the terms 'Fine' and 'Broad' we intend to promote fresh thinking about both their separate and their combined contributions. Fine cues – for instance, phonics and sight vocabulary – are traditionally familiar territory to teachers of reading. Broad cues – how books work, how stories are structured, genre and register – are not as readily recognized as having the same weight of relevance to word attack as the Fine. Our book, however, emphasizes their role throughout. Moreover, there is a danger that the Broad area, which should be a single unified area of study, remains fragmented, and distanced from the solving of a problem word. We hope our classification of cues will go some way towards rectifying this. Wells's recommendations (1986) for wide-ranging story-experience have provided us with strong support in this aim.

Fourthly, the Language/literacy postholder's question differs from the other three, being to do with the route through which the answers to those other questions reach the practising teacher. It is to do with effective communication. So the Postholder's responsibility in this is twofold:

- to circulate information about reading, both new and established;
- to show where it fits on the map of existing knowledge.

Her role is to be a bridge between theory and the classroom, and to try to ensure that no single piece of new research ever becomes such a bandwagon that other valid practices are abandoned; also, importantly, that ideas are filtered through a realistic evaluation of what works.

CAVEATS

There are some features of the book which perhaps need further comment:

- We have wrestled with the awkwardness of the English language in not having a neutral personal pronoun, and eventually decided to avoid the clumsiness of 'he or she', 's/he', and 'her or his'. Instead we adopt a purely stylistic convention, intended to be free of any value judgement, in which the child is 'he' and all supporting adults are 'she'.
- Of our quoted teacher–child exchanges, a great many (perhaps 50 per cent) are recollections, as near verbatim as memory allows, of actual exchanges between the authors and their pupils. Most of these were recorded at the time in brief summary notes only, with the total interaction carried in our memories. We are, after all, teachers not researchers. The remainder are orginations compiled to illustrate a point, and based on our years of experience of what young readers do and say.
- In turning the spotlight on to one-to-one interactions we aim to convey insights which are in fact a solid base for group and class work. Before you teach a multitude, first observe one.
- We fully acknowledge that this book does not include that important learning about reading which comes from learning about writing. The importance of the reading–writing link unfortunately has had to remain outside the remit we set ourselves for this particular book.

And a remit must be set, for as Huey recognized at the beginning of this century:

> To completely analyse what we do when we read would almost be the acme of the psychologist's achievements, for it would be to describe very many of the most intricate workings of the human mind, as well as to unravel the tangled story of the most remarkable specific performance that civilisation has learned in all its history.
>
> (Huey 1908: 6)

At the end of the century there are those who feel we still have some way to go: 'We are still a far cry from an answer. Mysteriously, we continue to read without a satisfactory definition of what it is we are doing' (Manguel 1997: 39).

In the meantime, however, the children cannot wait and teachers must teach. We hope to have made some contribution to their endeavours.

Rationale: the basics

THE THREE COMPONENTS OF READING

Let's examine that frequent plea: back to basics.

Reading involves not only 'reading the lines', but also 'reading between the lines' and 'reading beyond the lines.' These are the 'basics', these three intrinsic components. They have equal importance and are mutually supportive. From the beginning they are there.

It is their combined strength which transforms inert print into meaning. It is their fusion which puts life into what may be called the 'flattest' of those forms of communication which depend upon black marks upon a page. The composer can speak through musicians. The playwright can speak through actors. By and large, the author must abandon the book to speak for itself.

Were the author able to read the book out loud to a reader, we can imagine that the author would use all the skills of speech. The essence of the message would be signalled, not by the words alone, but by words combined with expressions, gestures, intonation and timing, and by feeding off the listener's reactions.

But readers left alone with the book do not have the benefit of any guiding performance. They are denied the flow of spoken language, a wealth of information to help them anticipate the author's meaning. Furthermore, those separate black marks on the page can acquire such towering importance as to be given exclusive attention. But this is tunnel vision. It inhibits receptivity to broader signals, for there is a stream of unseen information, if only the reader will attend to it.

In this book we shall develop an interpretation of 'basics', hingeing upon the relationship between the unseen information, which stems from experience of language and of life, and the seen information, which

Figure R.1   A basic model of reading

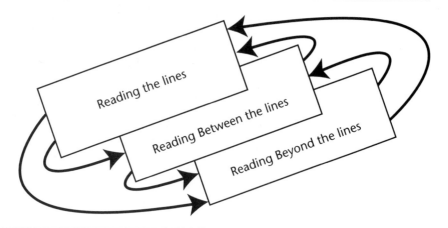

is the black marks on the page. Unseen and seen work in constant exchange with one another, in circular fashion. They cumulatively feed each other. Neither can stand alone, and it is academic which comes first.

Figure R.1 is the model of reading upon which we base our work.

The view of reading taken by the National Curriculum

A definition of reading as the successful integration of these three components is supported by the National Curriculum for Reading.

The report of the NCC working group, *English for Ages 5–16* (Cox 1989: Chapter 9), presented as its prime assumption:

> Reading is much more than the decoding of black marks upon a page: it is a quest for meaning, and one which requires the reader to be an active participant. It is a prerequisite of the successful teaching of reading, especially in the early stages, that whatever techniques are taught, or books chosen for children's use, meaning should always be in the foreground.

The Non-Statutory Guidance (DES 1989: para. 8.1) reiterates: 'When we read something we make sense of it ourselves, not just by "decoding", but by bringing our own experience and understanding to it.'

In the 1995 version, too, the Programme of Study for Key Stage 1 recommends that pupils should be taught sight vocabulary; phonic, graphic and grammatical knowledge; and contextual understanding, 'within a balanced and coherent programme'.

Furthermore, the National Literacy Strategy (DfEE 1998: 3) is 'based on a broad definition of literacy', which includes abilities 'to orchestrate a full range of reading cues (phonic, graphic, syntactic, contextual) to monitor and self-correct their own reading', and to coordinate skills across the three levels of text, sentence and word.

How welcome that we have a national policy that pulls together the work of the twentieth century, recognizing the elements of value from different reading theories that have prevailed over the decades, combining them into an inclusive model.

A journey around the basics – an illustration

The route that any reader takes in constructing meaning is circulatory, the three permanent components being visited and tapped for their information. This holds good, even for the developing reader.

By way of illustration, we would like you to observe with us the 'journey' taken by one young reader on one day as he read with his teacher. The route that Amandeep took to visit each of the three permanent components was unique to that page, that child, that situation: as is every reading experience.

At first he brought a one-dimensional view of reading to his story, which was one of the *Tales from Allotment Lane School*. (The words underlined were not read.)

Figure R.2	Amandeep's text

It was nearly half past ten, and that meant playtime. Laura looked out at the silver frost on the grass, and shivered. It was so warm and cosy in the classroom. 'I've got a headache', she said to Miss Mee, holding her forehead. 'I'd better stay in until it's better.' Laura's friend was Mary, and Mary heard her tell Miss Mee about the headache . . . She looked at the cold silver frost on the grass outside, then she looked at Laura. 'I've got a headache too', she said, making a dreadful face to show how it was hurting her. Sue looked at her two friends. She wanted to stay in and carry on with her colouring. 'Oh, Miss Mee', she gasped, suddenly holding her tummy. 'I've got a tummy ache. I think I'd better stay in too.' Asif held up his knee for Miss Mee to see the red scab. 'I fell over last week – I don't think I'd better go out either' . . .

Even though Amandeep was reading a story which took place in a classroom, a setting of which he had ample experience, and read some 90 per cent of the words correctly, he seemed not to have grasped the real implications of the incident. His comments betrayed a naive, literal interpretation of the children's attempts to avoid going out in the cold. He failed to draw on his own experience of some children's disinclination to go out during break, frosty morning or no! Moreover, although he was able to 'read the lines' in the passage 'She looked at the cold silver frost on the grass outside, then she looked at Laura', he mistakenly thought 'she' was the teacher, not Mary.

Amandeep had already been given some time to prepare, but when he read the passage aloud for the first time he was unable to read the words we have underlined. He paused at each one before moving on.

Now let us outline how the rest of the session went:

TEACHER: What were the children doing?
AMANDEEP: *They didn't want to go outside, and they didn't have to.*
TEACHER: Would Mrs Perry let you stay in if it was pouring with rain? [The teacher's first intervention was to relate Amandeep's imperfect understanding of the passage to a realistic situation of which he had ample experience – school life]
AMANDEEP: *Oh yes.*
TEACHER: Would Mrs Perry let you stay in just because it was frosty?
AMANDEEP: [laughs] No, she'd kick us out! [Amandeep has arrived at an insight into his own situation, but still does not relate it to the story]
TEACHER: So, what are these children doing?
AMANDEEP: *They don't want to go outside.* [Up to now, the teacher has not directed Amandeep's attention to individual words. She has led Amandeep to explore his own experience, but still this has produced only partial understanding]
TEACHER: Have a go at building that word. [Pointing to **tummy**, teacher selects a Finer cue (see page 16) chosen for its phonic regularity]
AMANDEEP: *'T-u-m . . . tummy'!* [This turns out to be the trigger releasing a run of connected meanings]
AMANDEEP: *'. . . ache'! 'Tummy-ache'!* [returning immediately to the top of the page] *'Head-ache'!* [Amandeep's spreading smile mirrors his delighted awakening to the children's ploys]
TEACHER: Now what do you think the children are doing? [The teacher confirms Amandeep's new awareness]
AMANDEEP: *They are coming up with excuses. They don't want to go out.* [laughs] *They wouldn't get away with it with Mrs Perry!* [This reflection shows that Amandeep has now made the connection between story and life]
TEACHER: Now read it all again.

This second time Amandeep reads without omissions, including **dreadful**, **colouring** and **suddenly**, which he could not get at previous reading. (Because Amandeep shares the author's intentions, now he is able to supply the missing 10 per cent of the words.)

TEACHER: [part way through, at line 5, Figure R.2] Now tell me, who is 'She'?
AMANDEEP: *Mary.* [Amandeep's reply is satisfactory indication that he has now made full meaning]

With the help of the teacher's considered interventions, Amandeep eventually drew information not only from the print on the page, but also from his own interpretation of events. With his experience in mind, we can now flesh out the components of reading shown in Figure R.1 in Figure R.3.

Figure R.3   **The basic model of reading further explained**

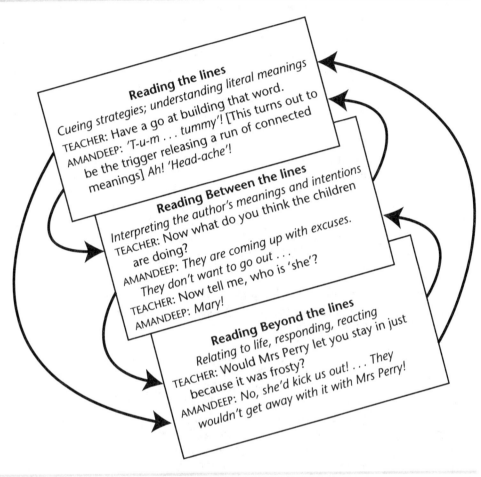

While the components of reading can be mapped out, there are a thousand and one permutations for the routes taken between them, each one unique. Amandeep visited all three permanent components, a journey every reader must undertake for reading to be reading in its fullest sense.

BASICS OBSERVED

The importance of observation

Amandeep grew to understand the passage because of the sensitive guidance of his teacher. It was her professional skill which enabled him to visit all the three permanent components of reading and tap each for its information. With Amandeep, as with all her children, she watched, and interpreted his efforts as positive attempts to gain meaning. Her timely and appropriate interventions arose from her willingness to attend so knowledgeably to Amandeep's responses that it virtually amounted to *him* teaching *her*. She was skilled in observation. This important skill lies at the very heart of teaching. Its value is not only in chronicling events but, more importantly, in spotting significance, and acting upon it.

In supporting the developing reader, the more we explore, the more there is to find, not only about the meaning of a child's approach, attitude, comments and 'miscues', but also how these are interlocked with his circumstances, and furthermore, with the texts he is reading. Watching and listening in an open-minded and informed way allows knowledge to be uncovered on where each learner is, relative to the wider scheme of what is to be learned. These insights into the smaller steps of reading development are not revealed by traditional assessment methods such as group tests of word recognition or sentence completion: for years, reading scores have *masked* a wealth of information. Observation is immensely valuable, because it allows the child to reveal his reading in sharper definition.

Observation for reading assessment in the National Curriculum

The National Curriculum for reading relies to a large extent on observation for reading assessment, complementing the blunt instrument of a reading score with the more sensitive measure of descriptive statements. In so doing, it acknowledges the observational skill which teachers begin to develop from the moment they enter the classroom. This welcome shift of emphasis – away from the ambiguity of reading scores, into observation – is to be applauded. It recognizes teachers' ability to pin the relevance of what they observe onto its rightful place on their mental map of the reading process. And so, observation, rooted in an understanding of reading development, *can* lead to effective action.

The language of observation

Reading has such a wide range of behaviours that only the language of observation will serve to capture them all. However, if observations of children's reading are to be shared, there has to be a common language. This is essential, because it is a rare happening indeed when two teachers together observe any child's reading or writing behaviour. Discussions between teachers on the relevance of what a child has said or done usually have to happen well after the event. Perhaps even discussion is not possible, and written records must serve. A unified language is needed, understood and used by the staff of any one school, between schools and across phases.

Teachers as a profession need to establish a shared precision of terminology. For reading teachers, the quality of their work depends on this because it enables them to:

- identify and describe all the facets of the developmental processes of reading;
- collaborate effectively;
- provide clear evidence for purposes of accountability;
- provide specific information to support allocation of resources and extra funds.

We need to move on from past imprecisions of a kind we would all recognize:

- one term used to mean various things (from a vague 'tries hard', to a purported technical term such as 'phonic approach');
- terms with close but different meanings, used as though interchangeable, for example 'paired/shared reading', 'build/blend', 'skim/scan';
- misunderstanding key elements because they are *not* named, for example the omission of the term 'cue' from the 1995 National Curriculum.

'CUE' – A TERM OF CENTRAL IMPORTANCE

The 1989 National Curriculum seemed to confuse 'cue' and 'strategy'. However, this confusion is not resolved through the 1995 expedient of dropping 'cue' altogether, an omission which does a serious disservice to the cause of clarifying the understanding of reading development. However, although the word disappeared, the element remained. Those outstanding signals from the pages of print did not go away because they were no longer named, a fact now recognized in the National Literacy Strategy's emphasis on 'orchestration of cues'.

The concept of the cue is so important that not only should the term be retained, it also should be further refined. The terminology we suggest includes a new term: 'tactic', and clarifies two existing ones: 'cue' and 'strategy'. This will help teachers to highlight each separate skill (tactic) of the developing reader on the way to being able to integrate them all (strategy). We define our terms in Figure R.4.

Figure R.4	Cue, tactic and strategy
cue	a cue is a clue as to what a word is;
	a cue is a signal from the text;
	a text is a fabric of cues
tactic	use of a cue by a reader
strategy	selection and integration of tactics;
	the reader's overall plan for getting meaning off the page

Amandeep, in his reading, began to develop a strategy of weaving together information, seen and unseen, to make meaning. Tactics were used to draw information from the cues on offer. Reading is a type of problem-solving, and the cues are the signals and information from the text, from which the reader can construct the meaning.

Amandeep's teacher was able to steer him towards the relevant cues because she had an awareness of the location of cues.

The location of cues

Being familiar with where cues are located in a text is crucial for both observing and supporting reading. Figure R.5 presents seven locations, knowledge of which is invaluable in practical work with developing readers.

Figure R.5   The seven locations of cues

A cue is a clue as to what a word is.
A cue is a signal from the text.
The text itself is a fabric of cues.

The words below in bold are the words signalled by these cues (underlined)

Location 1   A context cue close to the word

Example

A context cue closely preceding a word

'He looked at the <u>clock</u> to see the **time**'

A context cue closely preceding a word with several alternatives. Needs to be clinched by the phonics of the word

'He <u>heard</u> **cries**' (alternatives: **noises, sounds**, etc.)

A context cue closely following a word

'Bill **laughed**. <u>Hee hee hee</u>'

A context cue closely following a word, with one of several alternatives clinched by phonic cues

'**Cries** were <u>heard</u>' (alternatives: **noises, sounds**, etc.)

Location 2   A context cue in the text separated from the word

Example

A context cue some distance before the word. May also have a phonic clincher

'". . . hey!" She broke off. "What's that? You're covered in spots. <u>It's not catching, is it?</u> I don't want our Leonard getting it. It were bad enough when he had measles, chicken pox

	and whooping cough." She got to her feet. "<u>No, no</u>. It's just an **allergy**" '
A context cue some distance after the word. May also have a phonic clincher	'She lay there, very white just **alive**. "Take her to the castle, and tell the women to <u>look after her</u>" '

Location 3 A context cue separated by a page or more from the word	*Example* 'Wizard Blot made **mistakes**' [new page] 'Wizard Blot made a spell. The spell <u>went wrong</u>'

Location 4 A context cue from outside the text, for example the reader's prior knowledge May also have a phonic clincher	*Examples* 'The **pterodactyl** flew up' '**Jupiter** is the largest of the planets'

Location 5 Within the word: a phonic prompt, with a contextual clincher somewhere in text or picture	*Example* 'The <u>maths</u> teacher set them lots of hard **<u>multiplication</u> sums**'

Location 6 Picture cue with phonic clincher	*Example* 'Titch and his **tricycle**'

Location 7 Completely phonic No information from context or prior knowledge	*Example* 'This is a **cardinal** beetle'

Types of cues

Most of the 'cues' given in Figure R.5 as examples of the seven locations are not in fact single cues. They draw on more than one type of information, for example phonic, contextual, or prior knowledge (that is, Broad cues).

So the next thing we need to do is to look in more detail to specify just what types are available (Figure R.6).

Figure R.6	Types of cues

Broad cues

The reader knows what to expect from the genre (category)
The reader knows what to expect from the register
   (author's tone of voice)
The reader knows what vocabulary to expect for the
   subject matter

Broad and fine cues overlap

The reader uses all the cues on offer, including
• from the pictures
• from extended context
• from immediate context: the unbroken natural
   flow of language

Fine cues

The reader relates meaning and phonics
The reader uses own sight vocabulary
The reader uses punctuation to enhance meaning

The layout of Figure R.6 is designed to portray the equal importance of both unseen and seen information in enabling any word to be read.

The Broad cues are the unseen signals which draw on experience of life, language and books. The Fine cues are in the print on the page. Both Broad and Fine are vital, operating with equal force. Each merits some separate teaching, but of most use to the learner-reader is to discover their combined strength. His ultimate success as a reader will be through their integration.

When a reader encounters a difficult word, the knowledge provided by Broad cues includes:

• the genre of material he is reading (is it a novel? is it a maths problem? etc.);
• the author's tone of voice (is he aiming to amuse? is it in a formal register? etc.);
• the area of vocabulary to expect (is a story set in outer space or in an inner city? etc.).

These areas of Broad cue knowledge work in unison with the more widely known attributes of the Fine cues (sight vocabulary, phonics), which is why that area in Figure R.6 where they overlap is highly influential. This is where information gained from context is woven in.

David provides us with an example of how it works:

He was reading to his teacher about a boy who asked his father for a puppy. ' "Certainly not", said the father.' This word **certainly** presented quite a problem. His teacher silently considered whether this was the moment to introduce soft **c**. David read on, came back, and after a moment's pause read 'Certainly not'. His teacher asked him how he knew, and David replied 'That's what dads say.'

It matters not whether David was drawing on personal experience, or on book experience. What does matter is that his powerful knowledge of story, and of the likely nature of paternal response, together with his appreciation of the word's length, overrode the barrier of his ignorance of soft **c**. He had combined several cueing tactics – and we cannot know which one was the clincher – to fashion a successful strategy. This is the process the National Literacy Strategy refers to as the 'orchestration of cues' (DfEE 1998: 3). The following glossary of the terms it uses relates them to the types of cues identified in Figure R6:

contextual	all headings within the Broad cue box
graphic information	'the reader uses all the cues on offer, including pictures' (also diagrams, typefaces, layout, etc.)
phonics	'the reader relates meaning and phonics'
semantic	'the reader knows what vocabulary to expect from the subject matter'
syntactic	'the reader uses the immediate context: the unbroken natural flow of language'
word recognition	'the reader uses own sight vocabulary'

THE POSITIVE CUEING OBSERVATION SHEET (PCOS)

So far we have discussed observation, the necessity for speaking the same language, and cues. In order to draw these together in a form which provides practical support to a busy teacher, we have designed the Positive Cueing Observation Sheet to identify and record the cueing tactics in a working situation.

Evolving from the idea of miscue analysis, which focused on errors, this sheet highlights and records the emergence of positive development. It refers to a balanced cluster of reading tactics, some of which have not always been accorded their rightful importance. In fact, some have not been visible at all, masked within reading scores.

It details the 'small steps' of development missing from the National Curriculum documentation, in which each Level represents a wide continuum of development. Without care, therefore, there is some danger that a National Curriculum Level could be as blunt an instrument as a reading score. How informative is it to be told that a child is 'at Level 2', whether you are a parent, governor, or his next teacher?

We see the Positive Cueing Observation Sheet as a useful tool for the practising teacher, even in the busy classroom. It can provide an invaluable periodic 'snapshot', helping the teacher to focus on important reading behaviour, and assisting in the planning of subsequent action.

It analyses the detail of progression between the Level 1 description:

Pupils recognise familiar words in simple texts. They use their knowledge of letters and sound–symbol relationships in order to read words and to establish meaning when reading aloud. In these activities they sometimes require support. They express their response to poem, stories and non-fiction by identifying aspects they like

and the Level 2 description:

Pupils' reading of simple texts shows understanding and is generally accurate. They express opinions about major events or ideas in stories, poems and non-fiction. They use more than one strategy, such as phonic, graphic, syntactic and contextual, in reading unfamiliar words and establishing meaning.

Its use will be needed until Level 3, when children can

read a range of texts fluently and accurately. They read independently, using strategies appropriately to establish meaning. In responding to fiction and non-fiction they show understanding of the main points and express preferences.

We have numbered the items in the PCOS for convenience. This could misleadingly suggest linearity, and could even seem to imply that each item stands on its own. However, teachers will see that, purely as a means of assessment, it does separately highlight which are the strategies undeveloped by the child. Teaching can then focus both on attention to single tactics, and on their combined and fluent use.

We intend the statements to be straightforward enough for children themselves to understand, helping them to be aware of the skills in which they must progress. For children to take part in their own assessment in this way – 'I can read on into the next sentence to look for a cue' – is a highly useful form of metacognition, understanding how they themselves are operating.

Like the Broad and Fine cue areas which they reflect, the two inner pages are of equal importance, and are completely interrelated. The left side deals with attitude, experience, and the way a reader engages with the text. The right side deals with tactics for word identification. If photocopying, it is important to use A3 paper, so that the two sides can be opened out to offer a composite view of reading. They are designed to encourage a view of the child's reading behaviour as a whole. Combined, they prompt balance and unity, and we cannot stress too strongly that this fusion is the centrally important feature of our material.

Amandeep's teacher had this awareness of the interrelationship of all the tactics. She knew that if either side is neglected, left side equally as much as right, the balance is lost and problems arise. She knew that effort is often wasted by diverting enormous labour inefficiently to right-hand-page tactics, when use of some left-hand-page knowledge could be a catalyst. She recognized that with appropriate intervention, based on left-hand-page items, Amandeep could be helped to kindle his dormant understanding, leading him to 'relate meaning to phonics'.

The Positive Cueing Observation Sheet appears as Figure R.7. Some teachers' written observations are quoted to illustrate its use (page 22), and it will be helpful to read these in conjunction with the actual sheet.

Figure R.7   The Positive Cueing Observation Sheet (PCOS)

POSITIVE CUEING OBSERVATION SHEET

> 'They use more than one strategy, such as phonic, graphic, syntactic and contextual, in reading unfamiliar words and establishing meaning'
>   National Curriculum Reading Level 2 description (DfEE 1995: 28)

Name _____   Age _____

                                                                               Key Stage _____

Date _____

Class _____

Teacher _____

Material read:

Preparation time given: Y/N

Use this same sheet to record reading over several observations (for example half-yearly).
Make your dated entries in different colours.
Use material which challenges the reader at a rate of approximately five to ten problem words in every 100.
Try to allow the reader the normal preparation time.

READING REACTIONS

'Reading . . . is a quest for meaning and one which requires the reader to be an active participant.'

(Cox 1989: Chapter 9)

1 Initial attitude:

2 While reading . . .

(a) makes comments:

(b) asks questions:

(c) challenges/evaluates:

(d) non-verbal responses:

3 After reading . . .

– pupil initiated response/action:

CUEING STRATEGIES

> 'Reading is much more than the decoding of black marks on the page . . .'
>
> (Cox 1989: Chapter 9)

---

4 Uses own sight vocabulary efficiently:

---

5 Re-reads up to problem:

---

6 Reads on and returns to problem:

---

7 Gives reasonable alternatives to 'unknown' words …

   (a) using context:

   (b) using own knowledge:

---

8 Uses phonics to refine an attempt based on context:

---

9 Uses context to refine reasonable phonic attempt:

---

10 Economically uses phonics to generate words:
   (a) uses onset and/or rime to generate the word
   (b) uses first syllable to generate whole word
   (c) uses segments to build word correctly

Examples of teachers' written observations

Space within the numbered sections allows for descriptive comments or verbatim quotations, as well as a 'Yes/Sometimes/No' response. The speed at which some children read may mean that information has to be quickly jotted down on a pad at the time, and later transferred to the sheet.

To help clarify each behaviour, we offer the following examples of teachers' notes:

Left-hand page: Reading reactions

1 Initial attitude
Lisa mentioned she had read other books by the same author
Tessa's opening comment was: 'It's good, this'
Richard came grumbling 'Do I have to?'

2a While reading, makes comments
'They're having chips – we have chips'
'That wizard's not very houseproud'
'This book's only got 16 pages'

2b While reading, asks questions
Dave interrupted his reading with a questioning 'Eh? Why are they doing that?'

2c While reading, challenges, evaluates
'He should have cleared off when his dad got mad'
'I don't get this. It doesn't make sense'

2d While reading, non-verbal responses
Chuckled
Sara wanted to go on reading at end of session
Richard yawned, sighed, rocked
Word-by-word finger-pointing

3 After reading, pupil-initiated response/action
'Can I draw a picture?'
'Have you got another one by her?'
'Now can I make a little book about dinosaurs?'

Right-hand page: Cueing strategies

4 Uses own sight vocabulary efficiently
Sometimes: Having recognized **Samantha**, he successfully predicted
    next few words: 'came to my house'
Yes: There were no keywords among the words she couldn't read
No: If he gets one content word wrong, he misreads the following
    words, even though they are in his sight vocabulary

5 Re-reads up to problem
Yes: Chris is using this strategy nearly every time now
Sometimes: He could pick up the sense from my re-reading, but only once did he do this for himself. His style is too staccato. He is not thinking in chunks
No: Gemma stopped dead at each problem

6 Reads on and returns to problem
Yes: Seems to be doing this so well that I can't be sure how far ahead she has silently read, unless I ask her
Sometimes: Is aware of this principle, and can do it in a simple sentence. Can't retain larger units of meaning in more complex sentences
No: Tom read on . . . and on . . . and on, making no attempt to return, with enormous loss of comprehension
No: Chris never thinks of going past a difficult word

7a Gives reasonable alternatives to unknown words using context
Sometimes: In the sentence: 'They have heard strange cries at night', John read **noises** for **cries**

7b Gives reasonable alternatives to unknown words using own knowledge
Sometimes: He read **tackle** for **equipment** in the sentence: 'Anglers need the following equipment'
Sometimes: Jill read **wand** for **magic stick**

8 Uses phonics to refine an attempt based on context
Yes: Luke eventually read **cr-ies** after previously supplying **noises** and **sounds**
Yes: She corrected **terrified** to **scared** in the line: 'He was scared of the dark'

9 Uses context to refine a reasonable phonic attempt
Yes: She changed **hug** to **huge** once she had read to end of sentence: 'He gave him a huge box'
No: Persisted with **prŏt** for **protect** without taking any notice of the sense: 'You must protect the seeds from the frost'

10a Economically uses phonics to generate words, using onset and/or rime
Yes: He combined minimal phonic sampling (**str** . . .) with context to read **straight** in: 'Sally went straight home'
No: Said 'That bit's . . . eat', in **cheat**, but still was unable to use **ch** or context to get the word

10b Economically uses phonics to generate words, using first syllable
Yes: Built **sub** . . . then read whole word in sentence: 'The submarine went down under the black water'
No: Attempted to build beyond the first syllable of **concentrate** (**con** . . . **ken** . . .) without using following context: 'Concentrate on your work, boy!'

10c Economically uses phonics to generate words, using segments to build word correctly
Yes: Nicola put the syllables together successfully for **attention**
No: For **steam** he relied on the little word . . . **am** instead of the rime, . . . **eam**

Note: the fourth, blank, page of the PCOS may be used to note teacher action.

FIVE STAGES OF READING DEVELOPMENT

The next five chapters will describe five stages of reading development. In each the learner journeys between Reading the lines, Reading Between the lines and Reading Beyond the lines – the basics. He learns to draw equally on Broad and Fine cues. By presenting a consistent explanation of reading, and one which emphasizes the importance of cues, we hope to supply some support to teachers in their provision of the National Curriculum recommendation of 'a coherent and balanced programme'.

The name of each stage is meant as a description of its interactions between reader and supporting adult:

Bookbinding
Chiming in
Cue talk
Assisted reading
Branching out

These stages overlap, and no rigid boundaries can be set. The development of reading is a continuum (Figure R.8).

However, it is possible to see that there has been progress across each stage. At the beginning of each chapter we have resorted to the device of responsibility ratios to convey the impression of how much actual reading (or responsibility for saying the words) is undertaken by adult and child in any session. The first percentage given refers to the adult (for example *80* : 20).

In Bookbinding and Chiming in it is the adult who carries the main responsibility. Cue talk constitutes a significant switch, until in Assisted reading and Branching out the child is taking more and more responsibility himself.

We hope the following chapters will strike a chord with all concerned with the teaching of reading. There are many things which teachers intuitively do well. Their confidence is increased whenever they are able to relate what they do to sound principles.

Figure R.8   The continuum of reading development

Bookbinding
Books are shared and talked about with the child. *The adult is standing-in for the author.* The skills are implicitly demonstrated

95 : 5

Chiming in
The child now 'helps' the adult through the book. The adult is *still standing-in for the author*

80 : 20

Cue talk
Demonstration and explicit discussion of cueing strategies

60 : 40

Assisted reading
The adult helps the child through the book by continuing to teach cueing strategies. The child is taking over the responsibility for *standing-in for the author.*

40 : 60

Branching out
Independently uses cueing strategies

20 : 80   5 : 95

*Responsibility ratios: the percentages show responsibility for saying the words
(the adult percentage is the first figure)*

Chapter 1

Bookbinding

Books are shared and talked about.
At no time in Bookbinding will the child be asked to read aloud unfamiliar text.

Responsibility ratios 95 : 5 to 80 : 20

REASONS FOR BOOKBINDING

Rosie had no experience of books between the ages of 2 and 5. Jonathan's world was rich in literacy experiences. Moreover, there was a poverty for Rosie even in the quality of the spoken exchanges in which she was involved. Jonathan, on the other hand, was an active participant in a wide range of talk.

The development of these two children is charted in Gordon Wells's account of his research in *The Meaning Makers*. In this he clearly shows what can happen to two children from backgrounds providing starkly different language experience. He shows, for instance, that Jonathan had received no fewer than 6000 book and story experiences before he started school. So, from the moment he stepped into the classroom, he was able to make full use of what it offered, and forged ahead. Rosie struggled from Day One. Wells became convinced through his research that what children need

is a personal introduction to literacy through stories. Listening to a story read to the whole class is no solution, for they have not yet learned to attend appropriately to written language under such impersonal conditions. *For them what is required is one-to-one interaction with an adult centred on a story.*

(Wells 1986: 159)

Here Wells, in effect, has defined Bookbinding.
In this magic circle of child, book and adult, three minds – for we include the author's – become bound together in shared pleasure, warmth, discovery, meaning; three minds linked in the powerful activity

of storying. When a reception teacher plans her day, she should do so strengthened by the sound validation which exists for the inclusion of Bookbinding. So armed, there is no need for her to fear any challenges about time-wasting through reading with a child or about postponing the 'real work' of learning to read. Rather, she should be aware of the mechanism of that learning. Bookbinding is as 'real' as any other work, and forms the basis of later development. It is important for three reasons:

- *Story is essential to human experience.* Teachers and parents alike know how children drink-in stories with an insatiable thirst. Story is a universal, whatever the culture, whatever the generation, for reasons beyond entertainment and relaxation. Its purposes in making sense of the world are literally vital, as workers in many disciplines attest.
- *Talking about story expands and intensifies the experience.* Interaction in talk with another, about something read, is a communion reoccurring throughout life. Because such a bonding is both a literary experience and a life experience, it is not to be dismissed as a mere ploy for the learning-to-read stage.
- *The foundation is laid in Bookbinding for independent cueing tactics.* One-to-one interaction with a book is a route to literacy, developing the following elements:

Broad cues

- learning how to step out of the here-and-now to become engaged with the virtual reality of story;
- learning what a story is;
- learning 'book-language';
- learning to interact with a book – to question, respond, ponder;
- becoming familiar with well-known stories and rhymes;
- learning to anticipate and predict.

Fine cues

- beginning to acquire sight vocabulary;
- discovering that words are strings of sounds which can be manipulated; $\left.\begin{array}{l}\end{array}\right\}$ early
- becoming familiar with rhyme, alliteration, rhythm and repetition; phonological awareness
- beginning to recognize letters.

HOW TO BOOKBIND

Throughout Bookbinding, the adult, the chief performer, must stand in for the author, while the child, a reader only by proxy, is the attentive and responsive partner. There is never any direct tuition about cues, although much is absorbed by the child through being exposed to implicit demonstration. Bookbinding at home is as important as Bookbinding at school, and the following recommendations may help parents as much as teachers.

Here are nine things to think about when you Bookbind:

1 Show by what you say and what you do that Bookbinding is a priority.
2 Devote a significant part of the session to 'reading' the pictures.
3 Read *for* the child.
4 Make the author come alive.
5 Exploit the unique features of books.
6 Promote basic awareness of Fine cues.
7 Help the child to read Between the lines.
8 Help the child to read Beyond the lines.
9 Encourage the child to chime in.

1 Show by what you say and what you do that Bookbinding is a priority

Although the group and class sharing of big books is firmly established as a proven source of learning about books themselves, story and book language, it can never be a substitute for the personal exchanges of Bookbinding.

Incorporate it into daily literacy planning

- Use the classroom assistant to manage the volunteer-helper rota drawn up by the teacher.
- Use trained volunteer-helpers to Bookbind (see Chapter 6 for more on recruitment and training).
- Try to have trained help available during timetabled literacy work.
- Consider the use of Key Stage 2 children as story readers.

Make books attractive and accessible

- Make sure there are good books, accessibly placed.
- Keep up to date with new titles; have at least one member of staff responsible for this.
- Change book displays frequently.
- Promote books frequently, in addition to book clubs and book weeks.
- Introduce books by a particular author/illustrator, perhaps once a month in assembly.
- Consider inviting throughout the year a wide variety of local people to read (or tell) a story to small groups.
- Consider inviting secondary pupils (as part of their Personal and Social Education) to read or enact a story.

Make Bookbinding a warm, enjoyable, shared experience

- Find a comfortable place where adult and child can sit next to each other.

- Make your invitation refer to the book, and not to what you expect of the child, for example 'I wonder what this is all about?' rather than 'Bring your book to me.'
- Try to read the story as though each time was your first time (however familiar!).
- Become genuinely engrossed in the story and pictures for at least some of the time; not only does this relax the child, but it also then becomes a shared activity with a real purpose.
- Show interest and give undivided attention.

Involve the child in book choices

- Welcome the child's choices. Accept a repeated choice gladly; it is obviously important to the child. Keep these favourite books in mind in order to introduce more by same author/illustrator, or others which are similar.
- Look for opportunities to extend the child's choices.
- Be prepared to advise on suitable choices.
- Books will need to be read and re-read many times. Ideally this should occur spontaneously; if not, we need a range of ploys which will help to engineer it:
  - perhaps there is too big a selection of books available, so reduce the number of books around;
  - have a list of other adults ready, so that the child can share a particularly suitable book more than once;
  - claim to have such a bad memory that *you* need to re-read the book;
  - books on tape are an inducement for many children.

2 Devote a significant part of the session to 'reading' the pictures

If you give a significant part of Bookbinding time to 'reading' the pictures it signals to the child that this is an important part of reading. This conversation will:

- establish a habit of reacting to, and interacting with, books;
- allow the child to feel he 'owns' the book; he will feel in charge of its interpretation even though he is not as yet able to deal independently with words;
- develop the awareness that reading is a matter of searching out meaning from all the available information; consequently, the child will be encouraged to use picture cues as one crucial source of Broad information when later he begins to read text independently.

The following suggestions should help:

- Use the important resource of pictures in all books, not just picture books.
- Encourage the child to 'read' through the book first by telling the story from the pictures. This 'warms up' the reader, and activates vocabulary

about to be encountered. There are some children who have 'understood the game', and who will automatically use book language as they pre-tell the story. Others, less knowledgeable, who have first of all told the story in their own language, learn a great deal about book language when they then hear the author's words read aloud. For them, learning comes from the meeting between these two different languages applied to the same subject matter.

- Allow the child to continue over many repeated experiences until he is confident in telling stories from pictures.
- When *you* are reading the text on each page, linger over the pictures; they are not a mere adjunct to the 'real' story told by the text. The child will probably lead in this anyway, so do not deflect him.
- Dwell on details; search and explore the total 'landscape' of each picture.
- Talk to the child about the illustrator as a real person; introduce him/her to the child.
- Encourage the child to make links between the book and his own experience, including experience from screen and tape.

3 Read *for* the child

- Make sure the child is sitting in a position to follow each page.
- The better you know the text, the better interpretation you will give. If you possibly can, pre-read the book in order to plan a lively reading.
- Dramatize. If you are not careful you will simply be expecting the words to do the work for you. A flat read will not capture the author's message, any more than reading the lyrics of a popular song can communicate all that is conveyed by its live performance. So:
  - adopt different voices for different characters;
  - act out suitable words. This will help to extend the child's vocabulary. For example, take the words **shrieked** and **snivelled**. If these words are not yet known, he will find it difficult to understand them unless they are dramatized;
  - match the author's intentions with suitable intonations, to reflect, for instance, panic or delight;
  - use body language and gestures;
  - let yourself go, have fun (at worst, you can only make a fool of yourself).
- Hold the child's interest:
  - vary the pace;
  - lengthen words where appropriate ('slo . . . o . . . o . . . o . . . owly');
  - quicken the pace to reflect action and excitement;
  - vary the volume;
  - pause for effect;
  - use natural speech rhythm when reading characters' conversation.
- Read in meaningful, fluent phrases, not word-by-word, for example 'Off with a yowl, a wail and a howl, a scatter of paws and a clatter of claws' not: 'Off. with. a. yowl. a. wail. and. a. howl. a. scatter. of. paws. and. a.

clatter. of. claws.' The aim is to help the child develop an early appreciation of phrasing which will eventually lead him to a more intuitive
use of contextual cues. It will also help to prevent the later harmful
reading habit of halting at the end of a line even though it is not the
end of any phrase or sentence. Some of the time this can be supported
by moving the finger in a sweeping motion rather than word by word.
(We discuss finger-pointing in more detail in Chapter 2.)
- Build up a sense of expectation at a page end, especially before the final
  page when appropriate, relishing the ensuing punchline or revelation.
  The aim is to harness the child's natural inquisitiveness into the reading situation. Through the interest of each individual story the child
  will eventually develop an awareness of story formulae. From this will
  stem the ability to predict, drawing on Broad knowledge of story forms
  and on the immediate promptings of context.

4 Make the author come alive

We need to make sure, from time to time, that the child realizes that
there *is* an author. This understanding is in fact the seed which grows
into later critical skills – evaluating the craft of a writer, disagreeing with
something read. It may seem a long haul, and the dividends may not be
immediately clear – indeed they may not manifest for several years.
  Also, it prompts the child to see himself as a writer.

- Introduce the term 'author'.
- Make a habit of referring to the author one or two times each session.
  'Oh, good! You've chosen one by Shirley Hughes', or 'Oh! interesting;
  I've never read one by Shirley Hughes until now . . .'
- Point out the author's name on cover and spine.
- Pointedly look for information about, and a picture of, the author.
- Whenever possible, personalize, for example 'This author Roald Dahl
  used to write in his shed', or 'Val Biro really does have a vintage car,
  you know.'
- Show or remind the child that there can be several books by any one
  author.
- Seek out any dedication. Chat about who these people might be. (Did
  the author tell these tales as bedtime stories to his own children, for
  instance?)

5 Exploit the unique features of books

Unlike most electronic media, books can be sampled any time, any
where. They are portable. They can be revisited, pored over, lingered
over. And of course, they are constructed with features specific to the
world of print.
  Children need to be introduced to the mechanism of a book in order
to become competent and confident book handlers, and lovers of books
equally as much as of electronic media.

- Work towards making the children comfortable with the terminology, by making a habit of mentioning terms suitable for acquisition at this stage: cover, spine, title, dedication page, author, illustrator, publisher, etc.
- Exploit to the full any extra features such as lift-up flaps, pop-ups, sound additions, cutouts, picture-searches, bath-time books, etc.

6 Promote basic awareness of Fine cues

Fine cueing knowledge needs to be taught holistically, integrated within the reading situation, and not just in isolation, as a set of bolt-on parts. At this stage it comprises two main areas of development:

- the child begins to 'collect' a personal sight vocabulary;
- the child increases his phonological awareness through beginning to 'play' with words.

Good books provide the best motivation and the best medium for these developments, because the more a child enjoys a book, the more motivation it provides for pleasurable repetition. This promotes acquisition of sight vocabulary. Also a book which is enjoyable because its words are interesting enough to be playthings in themselves is an excellent medium for word scrutiny.

The child's natural delight in words as objects of interest in their own right leads him to make links between auditory and visual patterns of sound.

This supports the development of phonological awareness; hence the compelling need for books of good quality. (*Note:* there is more detail on phonological awareness on pages 34–6 and 37.)

7 Help the child to read Between the lines

Reading is like joining the dots in a dot-to-dot picture. The author provides the dots, the chunks of meaning. The reader has to grasp the dots and work at their links. In this way the reader's efforts are equal to the author's in creating an overall sense, which is why the reader may be said to be the 'co-author'.

At this first stage, being a dependent reader, the child relies heavily on the support of the adult reader to help him develop perceptions and interpretations. Discussion after reading will serve to promote a habit of reflection. Moreover, in the course of the reading itself, the adult will need to:

- signal each significant development in the story by means of stress, intonation, pausing, eye contact, laughter, facial expression;
- attempt to draw out a corresponding response from the child;
- ask open-ended questions such as 'What would *you* do?';
- talk about the links between the pictures and the text;

- talk about things which crop up in the text which you and the child had not anticipated from your preview of the pictures;
- talk about the opposite situation, too, when there is more in the pictures than is referred to in the text;
- question and make comments to tease out gently any implied meanings that the author has left understated.

8 Help the child to read Beyond the lines

Were the author present as storyteller, the narrative would flow seamlessly into discussion. There would be talk around what was in the story, and that talk would contain two main elements:

- growth in understanding of life and the world;
- evaluation of the tale and its telling.

Even without the author's physical presence to spark such discussion, these two elements are what we mean by reading Beyond the lines.

Reflection is as important at this stage as it is later. At this first stage the child benefits hugely from the adult's questioning attitude. A thoughtful extension to the reading of a book means that Bookbinding does not come to an end when the book itself comes to 'THE END'.

The post-discussion may include:

- appreciative questions, for example 'Did you like that?', 'What is your favourite page?', 'What is your favourite picture?';
- questions connecting the reader to the book, for example 'Have *you* ever. . . ?', 'Would *you* have. . . ?', 'Is that a bit like *your* dog/house/gran?'

9 Encourage the child to chime in

We need to avoid there ever being a Bookbinding situation in which the child is completely passive. We need to nurture each volunteered collaboration he offers. By gently indicating opportunities, and by responding warmly to his contributions, the adult can develop the child's understanding that Chiming in is a welcome development; in fact, the way forward.

Moreover, in order to chime in, the child has to make use of cues. So:

- Encourage and praise the child when he chimes in spontaneously, either because he is beginning to know some of the book by heart, or is using some cues.
- Pause when reading a well-known rhyme, an obvious rhyme, a refrain, a repeated phrase, a punchline, to create an opportunity for the child to chime in. Sometimes it helps to hold on to the previous word, with a questioning intonation: 'They huffed and they . . . ey . . . ey? . . .' Perhaps also include the opening sound of the next word, for example 'They huffed and they pppp. . . ?'

- Pause at the high point of a story, to give the child an opportunity to predict the outcome. This is a useful way of developing his awareness of Broad cues.

TWO WAYS TO DEVELOP PHONOLOGICAL AWARENESS

Incidentally – during Bookbinding sessions

During this stage the child needs to develop his appreciation of the fact that words are made up of strings of sounds, which he can manipulate. This appreciation is phonological awareness, and includes a recognition of patterns in language such as rhyme, alliteration and rhythm, and the understanding that through onomatopoeia at a very basic level, sound conveys meaning.

A great deal of this development occurs naturally and incidentally, as the child gradually increases his chimed-in contributions.

The words which he selects will very often be words whose interest lies as much in sound as in meaning: onomatopoeic words like **splash**; instances of rhyme; delightfully rhythmical phrases like 'Hairy McLairy from Donaldson's Dairy'; words which are fun to repeat – **bommi-knocker, didgeridoo**.

Such words may seem alarming as words for first learning, because of their visual complexity. However, an interest in words is a fundamental and necessary trait which must be encouraged, and the adult must join in with the child's relish of the words, her motives being to highlight and clarify their features. Look for these opportunities when choosing, from the wealth of good books available, books for school and class libraries. Their usefulness owes a huge amount to the happy coincidence that the very same literary devices which the authors employ – alliteration, rhyme, onomatopoeia – are those for which children need to develop an awareness. Helped by such good writing, children can be encouraged to develop their inquisitiveness about words, both in their own right and when incorporated into stories and rhymes. (Children learn best when they are at their most inquisitive – a fact which recalls Wells's observation that children's questions prompt their language development.) Their phonological awareness grows as they interrupt the adult's reading to comment: 'that rhymes'; as they play around with rhymes – 'smelly welly, smelly jelly . . .'; as they find some other word that begins like their chimed-in word; as they notice that all the words in 'Peter Piper . . .' start with a **p** sound.

During Bookbinding children also become interested in the look of the words on the page, and in letters and strings of letters – a natural interest which the adult must nurture. But it must always be remembered that of equal importance is the growth of the child's ability to hear and manipulate patterns of sound.

This early work on appreciation of sound (sound only, not sound-plus-print) is the essential foundation on which phonics for reading and spelling are built. Like all foundations it must be securely laid.

Armed with this knowledge, the supporting adult gains confidence to 'go with the flow' while Bookbinding, in two areas:

- confidence to watch out patiently for opportunities for phonological learning yielded by the books;
- confidence to utilize those opportunities appropriately.

And so phonological awareness develops bit by bit, like a photograph developed in the developing tray, through incidental input as we have just described, and through direct teaching.

Directly – through games and activities

Teachers and other adults helping within the school need to know about the child's developmental needs in this area. A glossary (Figure 1.1) summarizes some necessary technical terms, and Figure 1.2 outlines the steps of phonological awareness development through which the child will pass.

Figure 1.1 **Phonological knowledge: a glossary**

alliteration   use of the same consonant(s) to begin a series of words, for example 'Two toads totally tired tried to trot to Tidbury'

alphabet knowledge   knowledge of letter names and knowledge of alphabetical order

analogy   the same letter string appearing in different words

grapheme   the letter or letter combination which represents one phoneme

onomatopoeia   use of speech sounds to imitate an actual sound, for example 'the buzz of bees'

onset   the initial consonant or consonants of a word, for example *tr*-ip, *t*-ip

phoneme   each separate single sound in a spoken word

phonics   letter–sound relationships (phoneme–grapheme correspondences)

phonological awareness   'about recognizing, segmenting and manipulating sounds; does not involve any knowledge of print' (Harrison 1996: 29)

rime   the remaining segment of the word which follows the onset, for example **tr**-*ip*, **t**-*ip* (*Note:* a rime differs from a rhyme in that it also refers to the spelling. **Wait**, **bait** and **grate** all rhyme, but only **wait** and **bait** share the same rime.)

use of analogies   comparison of the onset or rime of one known word with the onset or rime of a new word, and deduction of the new word from that, for example **tr-ip** . . . **tr-ap**, **tr-ip** . . . **s-ip**

Figure 1.2	Steps in the development of phonological awareness

1 enjoying the sounds of words for their own sake
2 knowing what is meant by rhyme
   • can recognize a rhyme
   • can say when words don't rhyme
   • can make a rhyme
3 knowing what comprises the beginnings of words, i.e. onsets, because able to hear rhymes (**l.ip, dr.ip, ch.ip, k.ite, br.ight, h.eight**). Being able to say a whole word from hearing an onset ('Tell me something that begins with **dr** . . .')
4 being able to distinguish the separate phonemes of a rime (**i.p**) (**ai.n**) and of an onset (**d.r**)
5 being able to distinguish a vowel phoneme from its adjacent consonants: **c.a.t, c.o.t, l.a.st, l.ea.st**
6 beginning to be able to distinguish the separate phonemes in a word: **d.r.i.p, c.a.m.p, m.ea.t**

---

7 knowing how many syllables can be heard in a word (*Note:* this ability may be developed in parallel with the above abilities; it is not necessarily the seventh to develop.)

Finally, before we move on to look at letter knowledge, we offer some suggestions for activities to develop phonological awareness at this stage (Figure 1.3).

LETTER KNOWLEDGE AT BOOKBINDING STAGE: LEARNING SOME PHONEME–GRAPHEME CORRESPONDENCES

At this stage the children also begin to learn some letters, each child obviously learning at least the initial letter of his first name, and perhaps other letters with a personal significance. There will also be some planned direct teaching of a selected group of letters.

Children will have been *hearing* consonant blends as onsets, in I-spy and other games, and because it will bring children quite quickly to word-making, it helps to teach the graphemes for some initial consonant blends (onsets) as wholes, with wall displays linking them with pictures of objects and with collection tables.

There is a strong case for teaching **l**, **r** and **s** first – the reason being that these three letters team up with another seven letters – **b, c, d, f, g, p** and **t** – to give a total of 20 blends (**bl, br, cl, cr, dr, fl, fr, gl, gr, pl, pr, tr, sc, sl, sp, st, scr, spl, spr** and **str**).

So from the acquisition of ten letters, the child is given access to a total of 30 onsets, and these include virtually all the (onset) blends there are.

Figure 1.3	Early activities to develop phonological awareness

Awareness of rhymes

- all rhyming games
- poetry, nursery rhymes
- collecting/drawing groups of rhymed objects, for example 'our rhyming table'

Awareness of onsets

Based on alliteration

- I-spy – you may need to collect the appropriate objects. There will be a progression from single consonant to consonant blends
- list games, for example 'I went to market and I bought . . . The captain's cat is . . .'
- silly sentences, for example 'Six singing sausages sat swinging saucepans'
- collecting and/or drawing groups of objects beginning with same sound, perhaps producing their own 'Onset books', pages of pictures representing objects sharing the same onset
- odd one out – which two words begin with the same sound?
  box   cap   bed

Based on Spoonerisms

- semi-Spoonerisms: 'Say **lip**; now say **lip** without **l**; now make **ip** begin with **p**'

General

- telling a story in which you substitute a word with a changed onset or rime for the obvious word, encouraging children to chime in with the correction, for example 'So Goldilocks sat down on the big pear [chair!] . . . she climbed into bed and fell apeep [asleep!] . . . and suddenly her dod [dad] ran in!'
- clapping syllables
- clapping words in a sentence
- speaking like a Dalek, i.e. ev-er so slow-ly one syll-a-ble at a time

When children employ these in reading as prompts into a new word, and in their writing, the number of uses to which these are put far exceeds the number of letters which had to be learned.

Add to these a few two-letter words which are also reusable as rimes (use real words at first, for example **an**, **am**, **it**, **at**, **up**; actual words make for an easier start than free-standing 'nonsense' rimes), and the children have at their disposal some useful building blocks. Among these are some of the most easily formed letters for early handwriting (**i**, **l**, **t**, **c**).

Children's early introduction to written words should follow the onset + rime pattern, i.e. **c-at**, rather than **c.a.t.**, **fr-og** not **f.r.o.g.**

However, teachers must remain open-minded to those children who at first understand blending better if a word is 'topped' (as in **ca-t**), rather than 'tailed' (as is the recommended onset + rime way, **c-at**).

INTERDEPENDENCY OF BROAD AND FINE

We have just been describing the very necessary work of developing Fine cue knowledge. Broad cue knowledge needs attention in equal measure.

In fact, in making sure that Broad knowledge is developed the teacher ensures that the learning of the Fine will actually have more chance of success: it is the good soil in which Fine work may flourish. This is because the use of Fine knowledge is most effective when Broad knowledge has reduced the range of possibilities for any one word to a small number of realistic options. When the final clinching of a word is through the use of phonics, it can be the spark that kindles an immediate excitement in the child. This in turn promotes a willingness for further necessary, and separate, phonic work. Similarly, Broad awarenesses produce the conditions in which a basic core word can be recognized, because it has been anticipated.

In addition to what goes on in a Bookbinding session, there are also classroom activities promoting Broad cue awareness. For example:

- oral prediction activities
- picture sequencing activities
- drawing pictures and series of pictures after a story
- re-enacting stories.

BOOKBINDING AND 'THE BASICS'

We leave this stage with an overview (Figure 1.4) of how Bookbinding has supported the child in learning 'the basics', as shown on the basic model of reading Figure R.1.

Figure 1.4   Bookbinding and the basic model of reading

Reading the lines – cueing strategies

	Description	Examples
Broad		
Awareness of genre	The child knows there are lots of different types of 'stories' (texts). He knows what kind he is reading at any one time	Fairy story, stories of everyday life, nursery rhymes
Awareness of register (author's voice)	The child knows how to accommodate 'book language'	'. . . for he would surely swallow them up'; 'at the very edge of the forest'; 'a far-off land'; 'we must happy be'
Awareness of vocabulary	The child knows to expect sets of words appropriately associated	wishes-magic-spells-witches-princesses-forests-castles; kitchen-washing machine-bedroom-tidy-naughty
Awareness of structure	The child knows that stories have a beginning, middle and end; that some are based on well-used formulae	'Once upon a time there was a king who had three sons'; 'Fred had a big bike, Pam had a medium sized bike, and Titch had no bike'; nursery rhymes have rhyme and rhythm
Broad and Fine overlap		
Using illustrations	The child knows how to 'read' pictures to complement the text	The presence of the fox in *Rosie's Walk*
Using extended context	The child knows he may search widely through the story for clues to a specific word	Four pages after meeting **galley**, a reference to soup made Vicky realize it was a kitchen on a boat
Using immediate context	The child knows how to supply obviously predictable words	Rhymes, repetitions, punchlines, collocations (for example 'fish and chips', 'cloudy sky')

Fine

Relating meaning to phonics	The child knows how to complete a word from a minimal phonic start	'The Queen of hearts she made some t . . .'; 'Rock a bye baby on a tr . . . top'; 'one, two, thr . . .'
Recognizing core sight vocabulary	The child recognizes a personal sight vocabulary in different contexts and in different prints	He recognizes **car** from own name **Carl**
Using punctuation	The child knows the function of some punctuation marks	He knows that **Bang!** should be shouted

Reading Between the lines – interpreting the author's meanings and intentions

	Description	Example
	The child is able to understand author's meanings which are not stated literally; the child is able to interpret what is implicit	He comments on characters and situations: 'He's scared', 'That's naughty', 'He'll have to go to bed now'; understands that Willy the Wimp is going to body-build, and why

Reading Beyond the lines – relating to life, responding, reacting

	Description	Examples
	The child is able to make a connection between the story and his own experience	'My mum made me laugh about the monsters in *my* dream when she brought me a drink up' (about *Where the Wild Things Are*)
	The child is able to empathize with the characters	'My dad's always busy; so's my mum' (about *Not Now Bernard*)
	The child is able to evaluate characters' behaviour	'He should have cleared off when his dad got mad'
	The child has a sense as to whether characters, plot and setting are convincing	'One man couldn't sail that ship'
	The child is able to evaluate the skill and craft of authors and illustrators	'I *love* this bit'
	Child will return to the book, or choose another by same author/illustrator	

Chapter 2

Chiming in

The child's willingness to help with the reading increases.
At no time in Chiming in will the child be asked to read aloud
unfamiliar text.

Responsibility ratios 80 : 20 to 60 : 40

CHARACTERISTICS OF CHIMING IN

It is very difficult to say where Bookbinding ends and Chiming in begins, as the one slides almost imperceptibly into the other. It is essential that the activities in 'Nine things to think about when you Bookbind' (page 28) are practised throughout this stage too.

However, Chiming in is characterized by two important shifts, and the adult needs to be knowledgeable and supportive of what they are:

- *An increase in the child's contributions:* gradually but significantly the adult should decrease her contribution to the reading while encouraging the child to take up more and more opportunities for chiming in.
- *An increase in the child's awareness of Fine cues:* the adult will need to pay a certain amount of increased attention to developing the child's awareness of Fine cueing tactics.

RESPONDING TO THE CHILD'S CHIMINGS-IN

We now need to consider the adult's responses to approximations, those words the child gives when chiming in which are close to the actual text, but not identical with it. Let us look at Kate to see the value of these approximations.

Kate brought *Teddy Goes to the Seaside* to share with her mum.
Opening it page by page, Kate chortled at Teddy's exploits, pointing

to the pictures, telling the story in her own words. When she came to the page which read 'He had a delicious ice-cream', she suddenly licked the palm of her hand, and rubbed it all over the picture, saying with relish, 'Mmmmmm! Malicious ice-cream!' It was clear that she was recalling the book being read to her. She recognized the page and its information, and was able to produce an approximation to the text. Mum's response was to hug her, and to share the laugh, and only then to say: 'Mmmmm, he had a delicious ice-cream, didn't he?'

The pleasure and the humour of this event were remembered and recounted later by that mother, in the same way that parents so often celebrate the mistakes their children make in learning to talk. ('Do you know what she said today. . . ?') She did not overtly correct Kate's approximation, but simply repeated, warmly but quite clearly, the correct text version. She extended to the learning-to-read process the same easy tolerance she had given to Kate's learning to talk, avoiding any anxiety about the separate importance of literacy. She realized that experimentation is as important for learning to read as for learning to talk, and that experimentation will often produce approximations to accuracy.

A positive climate for alternatives

A positive approach to these approximations is to regard them as 'alternatives', valid attempts at making the same meaning as the author. This is some distance from regarding them as 'errors', or yet again as 'miscues'. To embody this positive view, the adult should aim for a climate in which:

- the child, in chiming in, feels sufficiently free to experiment, to try out alternative versions in search of the author's meaning;
- the child's alternatives are praised, for they are the first signs that the child is beginning to 'read' the author's intentions;
- whenever there is appropriate opportunity, some implicit reference is made to cues.

How to respond to alternatives

In order to flesh out these principles, Figure 2.1 offers some specific guidelines for their implementation.

Figure 2.1   How to respond to alternatives

Use the language and intonations of acceptance

CHILD: [reading *The Three Billy Goats Gruff*] '*Clip clop clip. Over the bridge.*'
TEACHER: Could be! Could well be! . . . er . . . I think this is the little goat. He goes [reading]: 'Trip, trap, trip, trap. Over the bridge.'

Accept and value the child's version

CHILD: '*It was a hot day.*'
TEACHER: It certainly was a hot day, I'm sure it was. [reading]: 'It was a sunny day.'

Be flexible in passing over close alternatives which do not distort the author's meaning
dad for **father**; **small** for **little**; **grin** for **giggle**; **dirty** for **muddy**; **scared** for **frightened**

Correct implicitly, using rephrasing

CHILD: '*The rabbit runned away quick.*'
TEACHER: [with continuing evident enjoyment of the story] Yes! 'The rabbit ran away quickly.'

Do not rush straight in when the child pauses
In that way you will promote the safe feeling that a pause for thinking is acceptable and valued. This is not easy from the adult's standpoint, but it is vital for the adult to learn how to stand back or there will be no development of independence in the child.

Discuss possibilities

CHILD: [reading *Little Red Riding Hood*] '*What big eyes you've got! All the better to . . .*' [pauses]
ADULT: Well, what does he do with his eyes? Yes! See . . .

Engineer opportunities for the child to chime in

ADULT: [reading *Hansel and Gretel*] 'It was a dear little house, *but* . . . it was the house of a . . .?' [pauses, questioningly, while pointing to picture showing the witch at the door]

USE OF FINGER-POINTING

One of the most widespread but unconsidered features of adult support in reading is finger-pointing. The way adults point at words is important from the word go, yet it is very rarely discussed. All too often it is almost a reflex action, without rationale, rarely varied in response to the changing needs of the child. However, because it can be a help or a hindrance, it is well worthwhile thinking carefully about the outcomes. All supporting adults need a range of techniques, because they must take account of variables such as the child's state of development, the text, and the child's attitude that day. They need to be aware of the following:

Productive uses of finger-pointing

- *To increase awareness of word-to-word correspondence.* Most young children do not appreciate that what they hear as a continuous flow of language is in fact a string of separate words. Often a child will have learned a page by heart, for which he cannot match individual words to the string of language heard. In this situation, pointing word-by-word is helpful, giving him written-to-spoken word correspondence.
- *To develop fluency.* A balance needs to be kept between showing word-to-word correspondence and demonstrating fluency. To do this the adult must emphasize the flow of language with a sweeping movement, left to right. This time the implicit lesson is that groups of words, although separate on the page, are to be phrased together. At later stages this can be used to encourage the child's own fluency.
- *To aid recognition of print as distinguished from other graphics.* This is a very early use, usually in early Bookbinding.
- *To aid early recognition of directionality.* This is another early technique, demonstrating that reading goes from top to bottom, from left to right.
- *To draw attention to the repeated appearance of frequent words.* For example, it can be used to count how many times we see 'Not now, Bernard!'
- *To demonstrate the need to read back.* For example, if the adult had read the giant's words in a booming voice, she might have found on reading on that his words were in fact described as being 'whispered'.
- *To support the closer examination of text.* For example: a classroom label – 'pens' – was spotted nearby as the words 'Ben opens . . .' were being read in a story. There was a discussion of how **pens** is part of **opens**, and a comparison of **pens** and **Ben**. Other opportunities occurred with the child's attention being drawn to the initial sounds (onset) of 'Rabbit **j**ump, rabbit **th**ump' for one child, and to the rime-section of the word for another child, for example 'Rabbit j**ump**, rabbit th**ump**' (also highlighting the rhyme).
- *To mark the left-hand edge of the line being read.* The child moves a finger of his left hand down the page line by line. This helps him to reduce a dependency on finger-pointing word by word, a step towards reading without any such support at all. It may also help a child out of a temporary difficulty in keeping his place. This technique is more likely to be used in Cue talk.
- *To help the child who always stops at the line end, not a sentence end.* This use is almost the equivalent of a nudge, employing only a brief

pointing, to help overcome disjointedness. Again, this is more likely to be used in Cue talk.

Note: It is important that the child still has a clear view of the rest of the page, so it is best if the finger points above any line of print.

Counterproductive uses of finger-pointing

Wrong messages can be inadvertently transmitted by those adults who unvaryingly and constantly point word by word. They are projecting a view of reading which the learners will take with them into the next stages. Those learners will:

- reflect a slow, cumulative, word-by-word view of reading;
- place an overemphasis on the mechanics;
- overconcentrate on complete word accuracy at the expense of comprehension;
- adopt a slow, staccato style of reading, a 'metronome' style, which prevents continuous sense from getting through;
- resist reading on and reading back, reflecting a view of reading as a linear progression.

DEVELOPMENT OF PHONIC KNOWLEDGE

Incidental development – during a Chiming in session

Here at Chiming in, the explicitness of the adult's interventions are 'moved up a notch'.

- Whenever the adult is aware that there has been some letter-learning by the child, she should use opportunities to draw the child's attention to these letters in the reading situation, for example 'Do you remember when Miss Mullarkey showed you Fireman Fred yesterday? Well, look at "Freddy Fox" here. There's an **f** here again, look, and again.' This should only be done at suitable points, so as not to destroy the flow of meaning.
- The adult can boost the child's confidence by drawing his attention to certain words which he read for himself. These often provide opportunities to make links with his letter knowledge.
- Other links will be possible between the text and the child's current writing experience.

Direct development – through classroom activities linking children's oral knowledge to print

- *Orally.* Classroom activities will focus on increasing children's skills at segmenting words, now in a greater variety of ways, for example **Spot** might be **Sp-ot**, **S-pot**, **Spo-t**. As just one example for instance, now they can begin to manage full Spoonerisms, progressing from the semi-Spoonerisms with which they played in Bookbinding ('Say **lip**. Now say **lip** without **l**. Now make **ip** begin with **p**.'). For full Spoonerisms the children are asked to swap the onsets of paired words, for example 'pink jelly' – 'jink pelly'.

- *The written forms of words*. From this oral understanding children should be led to observe the same manipulations with written letters. As children play at making words they are becoming involved in the manipulation of the various 'blocks' which comprise the word:
  - onsets plus rimes, for example **l-og**, **st-amp**
  - onsets, plus 'middles' plus 'ends', for example **l-o-g**, **st-a-mp**.
  A variety of apparatus can form the basis of this play at making words: word-wheels, word-slides, computer games and, importantly, plastic letters.
- *Use of plastic letters*. For many learners the abstract and fleeting qualities of phonological awareness make it a difficult kind of knowledge to convert to the concrete and static qualities of print. Such children are helped, if, as they are working to develop phoneme awareness, they are given something 'concrete and tangible to work with' (Bryant and Bradley 1985: 122). The use of plastic letters helps to make the manipulation of phonemes something which is quite literally graspable. It can clearly be seen which letters need to move and which stay the same, as 'families' of words are produced sharing either an onset or a rime.
  The benefits of plastic letters may be summarized as follows:
  - they turn the abstract into the concrete;
  - they help manipulation of otherwise abstract concepts;
  - they provide control for the learner over phonemes;
  - they promote discovery;
  - they are graspable;
  - they are colourful and attractive (but avoid colour coding);
  - they allow errors simply to disappear – no crossing-out;
  - they free learners from the extra task of letter formation;
  - they provide a relaxing game element;
  - they move easily.

Magnetic letters have similar advantages for groupwork when using vertical surfaces.

INCREASING LETTER KNOWLEDGE: PHONEME–GRAPHEME CORRESPONDENCE

During the Chiming in stage, children should complete their learning of the single grapheme–phoneme correspondences represented by the 26 letters of the alphabet, adding some of the most frequently used digraphs, for example **ch**, **sh**, **th**, **oo**, **ee** and **ar**.

There is more detail about vowel and consonant learning in Chapter 4 (Assisted reading) under 'Phonic knowledge within reading' (page 107).

However, it is interesting to note here also that, when consonant blends are introduced, it is much more productive – and saves a great deal of labour – to concentrate on initial blends (onsets) rather than final. Consonant blends in a final position do not often cause a problem for the reader, as they are handled via a process of anticipation: by the time the reader has read onset + middle + first-consonant-of-the-final-blend, he has usually predicted the whole word accurately, and supplies the final consonant.

Health warning

We leave these sections on phonological awareness and letter knowledge with this piece of advice from Adams, following her commissioned researched answers to the questions posed by the US Department of Education (Adams 1991: 371): 'Is phonics a worthwhile component of reading instruction? If so, why? And how might such instruction be most effectively realized?'

> Code instruction may be likened to a nutrient, a basic building block for the growing reader . . . First, the ingestion of the proper amount of such a nutrient is critical to students' potential development. Second, we realize its proper metabolism will not occur in the absence of a balanced diet. And third, we find that – however healthful it may seem – we must be careful not to dish up too much . . . Extra phonic calories do not enhance growth. They are kept as unnecessary and burdensome tissue or quickly flushed as waste. Worse still, the child may become groggily sated before getting to the other necessary and complementary items on the menu.
>
> (Adams 1990: 50–1)

Adams's analogy makes relevant the following reminder about the interdependency of Broad and Fine: *just as in Bookbinding, it is important to maintain activities to develop Broad cueing knowledge, such as:*

- *oral prediction activities,*
- *picture sequencing activities,*
- *drawing pictures and series of pictures after a story, and*
- *re-enacting stories.*

AN OVERVIEW

The following menu of recommendations for a Chiming in session (Figure 2.2) also serves as an overview of the suggestions to be found in this chapter and the previous one. Both chapters encompass what is overly simplified when referred to as Shared reading.

Figure 2.2   A menu for Chiming in

- Involve the child in the choice of the book.
- Read the pictures.
- Make the author come alive.
- Exploit the unique features of the book.
- Help the child to read Between the lines.
- Help the child to read Beyond the lines.
- Read the book for the child, without any finger-pointing. The adult knows that the story is in a book, but she endeavours to make it sound as if she is telling a story.
- Encourage the child to have a go at a similar reading, promising to chime in yourself whenever necessary.
- Use a range of finger-pointing techniques, as appropriate.
- Encourage child's closer attention by encouraging him to finger-point as *you* read, in order to:
  - engage his close attention
  - increase his awareness of word-to-word correspondence
  - increase his awareness of sentence pattern rather than line breaks.

'BUT HE DOESN'T WANT TO READ!'

We seem to have been describing an idyllic situation in which the young reader is forever clamouring to be read to! Common sense and experience tell us that this may not be the case. Some ploy must be found to entice the reluctant reader. Some of the following work some of the time:

1 the adult claims to be too tired; she needs the child's help;
2 the child is asked to 'read' to a younger child;
3 the adult claims to be unable to find her glasses!
4 the adult suggests that each take a character in the story ('You be the Wolf. Show me how he gets fiercer and fiercer . . .).

However, all of these depend in the first place upon the long-term establishment of an ethos in which reading is seen as a valued occupation; there is no quick fix for this, and the roots stretch back to babyhood.

Chapter 3

Cue talk

The child takes on more responsibility for reading the words.
The adult involves the child in Cue talk.

Responsibility ratios 60 : 40 to 40 : 60

A SHIFT IN ROLES

'Cue talk' is the turning point where Chiming in begins to turn into
independent reading. It is during this pivotal stage that roles are
exchanged as the weight of responsibility tilts from adult to child. As the
child is more willing and more able to take on responsibility, so the adult
responds by introducing explicit instruction on ways to read some, but
not all, unknown words. This shift is immensely important, with implications for the child not unlike those of moving from understudy to
leading role, and this moves him into a new confidence band. Witness
Sean, who had experienced an important and exciting event:

> 'I can read now,' remarked Sean.
> 'Can you?' said his teacher.
> 'Yes. It happened last Monday.'
> Sean had enjoyed a few moments of unsupported reading, a few
> moments which had given him a new perception of himself as an
> independent reader, bringing an accompanying surge in self-esteem.

RECOGNIZING READINESS FOR CUE TALK

Sean's announcement is unusual in its precision, although many parents
and teachers use similar global statements, including 'The penny's
dropped' and 'It's suddenly clicked with him.' Such statements suggest
that progress has happened overnight. In reality, these landmarks are
made up of a steady accumulation of smaller steps of growth, and this is
the case during the transition from Chiming in to this stage. Although

small and often undervalued, the signals are there, waiting to be observed, provided the adult is alert to their rightful significance. (Interestingly, they are sometimes recognized but reported negatively, a misunderstanding which reveals how much they have been undervalued: 'He's not reading, he's just learned it off by heart', 'He doesn't know all the words yet', and 'He's got lots of books but he only looks at the pictures'.)

The child is ready to move into Cue talk when he is doing most of the following:

- during Chiming in he is more willing to take the lead: 'Let *me* read this!' (At times he seems almost to be pushing the adult aside);
- his choice of books is widening;
- he spends more time with books;
- he gets more words right;
- his secure sight vocabulary is increasing (i.e. he recognizes certain words wherever they appear);
- faced with a text he knows orally by heart, he can now point to words with correct correspondence;
- within some words he can recognize smaller words (for example **rain** in **train**, **eat** in **seat**, **all** in **ball**);
- within some words he can recognize letter strings (for example 'That word [**stop**] begins like my name [**Stephen**]');
- through awareness of analogies, he is beginning to generalize (for example because he knows **look**, he is able to read **cook**);

(See also Figure 6.3, Signs of progress, pages 158–9)

These behaviours are evidence of an exciting development already under way. The child is beginning experimentally to tap into the cueing system. He is now beginning to realize the system, the game plan.

DUAL DEVELOPMENT

To take this further the child must develop on two fronts:

- a detective-like approach to unknown words;
- an ability to analyse and articulate what he is doing.

Detective-like approach to unknown words

Throughout Bookbinding and Chiming in the child was securing a small store of sight vocabulary, and some knowledge of letter sounds. Now he is developing an understanding that he can deploy this secure knowledge to tackle unknown words; he has knowledge which is transferable. For instance, he might deduce the whole phrase 'fish and chips' from having met **Chip** in Oxford Reading Tree, or he might reason out **football** from knowing the sound of **f**, and the **all** in 'all the king's men'. Moreover, his final estimation of a word is based as much on what will hold meaning in context as on what the word looks like. He is, in fact, discovering how to play detective, searching for evidence drawn both from the print on the page and from his expectations, to decide on a meaning. He is realizing that, from somewhere within himself, he can find the knowledge. He is also realizing that this secure knowledge generates new knowledge. He has a new sense that he can take some control of his learning. This is a development which the adult must now pick up and extend.

Ability to analyse and articulate what he is doing

Equal in importance to the development of a detective-like approach is the complementary development of an ability to talk about it. The child is learning that reading is a problem-solving activity, and, as with any problem-solving activity, there is a need for an evaluation of the 'working'. In mathematics, for instance, the working is valued along with the answer. If the process is shown to be sound, the child's thinking is confirmed, despite any final wrong answer. This will support him in future situations when, faced with a similar mathematical problem, he will not be deterred from using what is basically a sound method. Similarly in reading, the adult owes it to the learner to confirm when he is on the right lines. Such consolidation will strengthen the bond between adult and child and improve his self-image.

Throughout the Cue talk stage the child must move gradually from his vague awareness of cueing tactics at the beginning, towards the goal of the next stage – being so knowledgeable about cues that he is able to talk through his working. (Development of phonic knowledge continues throughout the Cue talk stage, but has not been included in this chapter. The detail is discussed in Part 5 of the next chapter, under 'Phonic knowledge within reading', page 107) Eventually, the child needs to know the game so well that he could be an 'instructor' himself. (In fact, employing a young reader as an 'instructor' in a reading partnership can give him confidence because he is consolidating his own knowledge while helping a less proficient child.) If we cannot get children to the point where they can verbalize their thinking, we are not developing independent readers.

The agent for this dual development is discussion, as the adult involves the child in talking about cues – in Cue talk.

CUE TALK: THE ADULT'S ROLE

Cue talk is a type of problem-solving discussion which should take the place of those drawn-out silences which occur whenever an adult, misunderstanding her task, simply sits and waits overlong for the child to read any difficult word. Once the adult has realized that her task is more than 'hearing' reading, discussion can transform a pressured situation into a collaborative search for meaning. Accordingly, the child comes to understand that, rather than an examiner, the adult is his personal adviser supporting him through a puzzle.

During the previous stage of Chiming in, the adult accepted 'alternatives', words which were appropriate in meaning but which were, nevertheless, alternatives for the word on the page. Now in Cue talk her positive response becomes more focused. Although she still makes the child feel that his alternative has been respected, now she confirms his cueing routes; her use of appropriate technical language helps to consolidate his thinking. Of course, the explanations of tactics and strategies (see Figure R.4, page 13) will need to be phased in gradually, as she directs his working to the other cues which are available to deduce the author's actual word.

To be meaningful, her explanations should be guided by what the child's alternative or word attempt (for example **str** for **straight**) reveals about his cueing awareness. She needs to consider these questions:

- Was the attempt confident or hesitant?
- Was it whole-word or a tentative sampling of a part?
- Was there evidence of some use of cues?
- Was the child satisfied with a meaningless alternative, or did he attempt to self-correct?
- Did he make any comment on his own strategy?

The adult's willingness to build from these sources of information is vital if the shift in her role taking place now at this third stage is to be effective.

Two requirements for the adult to be successful

- *Knowledge of cues.* For Cue talk to be effective, the adult must know about cues (see Figures R.5 and R.6, pages 14–15 and 16). This is essential knowledge, because the focus of her curiosity must be on what cue-using skills the child has developed when looking for information about a word. She needs to know what it is he knows, and what it is he needs to know, steering him towards keeping a balance between Broad and Fine cues.
- *An enquiring mind.* She will need to be curious to explore what is going on in the child's thinking, a far cry from the over-simple attitude which looks merely for the child to get it right. She needs to be interested in the thought processes of the child. Rather than saying 'that's right' and 'that's wrong', she needs to be saying: 'that's clever, I see how you worked that out; the author could have used your word there.' She has to be excited and enthused by what the child is doing.

By adopting such an enquiring stance towards reading as a problem-solving activity, a supportive atmosphere is produced. This safe and tolerant atmosphere is necessary for the child to feel secure to make mistakes; mistake-making is a necessary ingredient of all learning, and one which provides data from which the adult is able to select the opportunities for teaching.

CUE TALK

Having freed the child to make 'mistakes', then the adult must be ready with appropriate responses. When the child offers an alternative, or a word attempt, the adult must decide whether her response will be:

- to maintain the flow of language by giving the word;
- to focus on the child's reasoning;
- to lead the child into deeper study of available cues.

We have coined the terms 'focus words' and 'study words' to be of practical guidance, and to arm the adult with the understanding that different types of alternatives and word attempts require different types of support.

Focus words

A word is chosen as a focus word when the child's alternative clearly demonstrates some use of cue knowledge. The adult then puts that knowledge into words on his behalf.

Take the following examples in which three different children misread **straight** in the sentence: 'It stood straight and tall' (which was accompanied by a picture of a sunflower). In these examples, **straight** is the focus word.

The adult's response to the three alternatives might be as follows:

CHILD A: *'It stood **nice** and tall.'*
Type of cue used: the alternative **nice** for **straight** clearly shows the child's intuitive grasp of immediate context.
Adult's aims: to praise the use of contextual cue, to verbalize the child's working for him, and to supply the word and regain the language flow.
Adult's response: 'Yes, **nice** makes sense there. The author could have used that, but actually he used **straight** . . . "It stood straight and tall".'

CHILD B: *'It stood **str** . . . and tall.'*
Type of cue used: the attempt **str** . . . for **straight** shows the child's overreliance on letters divorced from content.
Adult's aims: to praise the use of a letter-string cue (phonic prompt), to verbalize the child's working for him, and to supply the word and regain the language flow.
Adult's response: 'That's very clever, to notice **str**. It says **str** . . . **aight**: "It stood straight and tall".'

CHILD C: *'It stood **still** and tall.'*
Type of cue: the alternative **still** shows a child drawing on both letters and meaning.
Adult's aims: to praise the combined use of contextual and letter cues, to verbalize the child's working for him, and to supply the word and regain the language flow.

Adult's response: 'Oh! you're nearly there. That's hard luck, because you're thinking so well about that word. **Still** does make good sense, and it does have **st** at the beginning. Actually, it's **str . . . aight**: "It stood straight and tall".'

The adult focused on the three alternatives **nice, str . . .** and **still** because they showed the children making some sensible use of cues. This provided the adult with an opportunity to feed back to them those revealed strengths. The choice of any focus word depends on the features of the alternative given by the reader, which should afford the adult opportunity to praise his cues and formulate his thinking.

At the outset of Cue talk the child has an intuitive grasp of what has led him to any attempt, but cannot yet articulate this thinking. The adult can only gather the extent of his knowledge from his attempts and alternatives. Her job is to feed that information back to the child, articulating his thinking for him, aiming to raise his awareness towards that later stage when he can use cueing tactics with deliberate purpose.

How many focus words per session?

In any single ten-minute session there might be one, two, or maybe three such focus words. Any other words which the child finds at all difficult will be immediately supplied by the adult, thereby maintaining the flow of language and overall meaning, and, crucially, ensuring that a sense of pleasure and success is retained. It is not possible to give hard and fast numerical advice about how many words to focus upon, but a useful rule of thumb is:

• Do not interrupt the flow of the text too much.
• Do not erode the sense of enjoyment.

Study words

In time, dependent on the child's understanding, one focus word per session will be turned into something more: a study word. As a focus word, it will have given an indication of a certain level of sensible cueing by the child. In selecting it as the study word, the adult will be aware of its potential to improve the child's awareness of the wider range of cues on offer.

The adult should lead the child to think about those other cues which he had apparently not considered in his original attempt, as the following examples demonstrate. Here, she has chosen **straight** as the study word. She begins by giving a focus response but stops short of supplying the word.

CHILD A: *'It stood **nice** and tall.'*
Adult's aim: to add a letter cue, and link it to the contextual cue used by the child.

Adult's guidance: 'Yes, **nice** makes sense there. The author could have used that, but let's see what he did use.' She puts her thumb over the ... **aight** section of **straight**, in order to focus on the phonic prompt provided by the initial cluster **str**. 'That says **str** . . .'

She re-reads the sentence, supplying only the **str** . . . for the word: 'It stood **str** . . . and tall.'

She pauses, waiting for the child to supply the word now that he has had this dual phonic and contextual support.

If the child is not able to come up with the word, she might point to the picture, in order to elicit help from that source of information also.

And if he still cannot supply the word, no more problem-solving work should happen at this stage: the adult should supply the word and move on.

CHILD B: *'It stood **str** . . . and tall.'*
Adult's aim: to point out contextual cues, eventually linking back to the letter cue the child did use.
Adult's guidance: the adult will cover the word, or maybe by turning the book over, the whole page.

She will re-read the sentence saying the word **something** in place of **straight**: 'That's very clever, to notice **str** . . . Listen: "It stood **something** and tall." Don't worry about the letters for a minute. Let's see if we can think of other words to make that sentence work. How many can we think of?'

She re-reads, again saying **something** in place of the missing word: '"It stood **something** and tall" . . . It stood . . . ?'

She is willing to write all the alternatives down, praising any that make sense, for example **big**, **high**.

After that, if the child is still searching for the sense, she might also turn to the picture, and remind him of his attempt which correctly used the phonic prompt **str** . . . , re-reading the sentence with only **str** in place of the whole word: '"It stood **str** . . . and tall".'

If, after all this, the child does not respond with the word **straight**, the adult should supply it and move on.

CHILD C: *'It stood **still** and tall.'*
Adult's aims: to refine the letter cue and then combine letter and context cues.
Adult's guidance: 'Yes, **still** does make good sense, and it does have **st** . . . at the beginning. But look at these *three* letters here: **str** . . . These three are the ones to concentrate on. You looked at two, but if you look at the three you will get a better clue.'

She re-reads the sentence with **str** . . . in place of the whole word. 'It stood **str** . . . and tall.'

If the child does not get **straight** at this point, she works with him as she did with Child A on page 54.

As in both the examples above, she might draw on pictorial information if needed.

Criteria for choice of study word

One of the adult's important concerns is to ensure success, and this means care in the selection of the study word. It is unlikely that the word can be pre-chosen, as the child's reaction can rarely be predicted. If a wrong word *is* inadvertently chosen by the adult, and the child is unable to take advantage of the cues on offer, even with guidance, then she should quickly bale out by supplying the word, and move on.

The adult must realize that she is not there to check that the child gets the words right, nor to involve the child in a battle, nor to censure failure. She is there to try to select a successful learning opportunity, based on these two factors:

• the child's initial attempt reveals some good cueing knowledge;
• features in the word or text offer potential to extend his cueing knowledge.

How many study words per session?

We suggest no more than one study word per session. If a child has one reading session per day, each with a study word, then he has five detailed learning intervals per week, sufficient usually to move him forward at a pace that ensures he remains motivated while continuing to learn. If more is attempted, there is the danger that the supportive nature of the sessions, so carefully nurtured, could come to be destroyed. We need to maintain the confidence, enterprise and enjoyment which characterized Chiming in, when the adult was primarily a demonstrator.

Caught or taught?

As teachers and parents will recognize, there are those children who need hardly any guidance, spontaneously registering for themselves their process of deduction, often with some excitement. For others, processes and cue use must be taught, and for these children talking about cues is especially valuable. Among these there are some children whose development is blocked only by their failure to grasp that there is any overall game plan at all. For these it is not helpful if their exclusive strategy is to go straight into the more obvious Fine cues, tackling words phonically. Rather, they need to have the *whole* game plan demonstrated – Fine and Broad cues, in balance. Often this can be enough to clear the reading block. We must always remain aware that among those children assessed as having a reading problem, there will be some for whom a lack of overview constitutes the central problem. This can even be the case for some of those identified as having specific learning difficulties (dyslexia).

MAKE-UP OF A CUE TALK SESSION

A Cue talk session is a kaleidoscope of the following activities:

- the child is reading some of the text successfully by himself;
- the adult is reading for the child;
- both adult and child make comments about the story;
- the child is reading some of the text with frequent alternatives;
- the adult is talking about cues for two or three focus words;
- the adult is extending the child's cueing knowledge via a study word.

Also, there will be reference to other phonic instruction outside the Cue talk session, instruction which has already taken place or will take place as a follow-up.

Each session contains all of these, but each time they fall together in a unique composition. So far we have concentrated on those intensive focus and study interactions, but the other elements are equally important.

Figures 3.1 to 3.6 describe each activity, and together are intended to provide an overview of all the ingredients of a Cue talk session.

The training for all supporting adults needs to be more precise than in the two previous stages. Cue talk demands that the adult possesses sufficient flexibility and awareness to be able to switch between active and passive roles – part demonstrator and discussion-prompter; part listener and information-gatherer. It also demands knowledge of cues, as we have described earlier in the chapter.

Figure 3.1	**Child reading successfully by himself**

Child's action: reading successfully by himself with no significant errors

Adult's contribution:
- encouraging, by:
  - body language
  - approving murmurs, for example 'Mmmm . . . ah-ah!'
  - praise – constant, brief, sotto voce, for example 'Lovely! Yes . . . keep going.'

Positive feedback on successful reading is a vital ingredient in this learning process. All too often a child hears adult comment only when something has gone wrong.
- weaving in comments Between and Beyond the lines, for example:
  - 'I never thought he'd catch him'
  - 'Can you see the little dog hiding round that corner?'
  - 'Do you think he was naughty?'
  - 'Did you like that story?'

The adult needs to maintain a balance between comment on the child's performance and comment about the story itself.

Figure 3.2	Adult reading for the child

Adult's actions:
- making sure the child is sitting in a position to follow each page;
- dramatizing;
- holding the child's interest;
- reading in meaningful fluent phrases, not word by word;
- building up a sense of expectation at a page end;
- encouraging and praising the child when he chimes in;
- pausing at suitable points to encourage the child to chime in.

Child's contribution:
- following the text;
- chiming in when he can;
- commenting on story and pictures;
- sometimes commenting on cues.

This activity allows for:
- *the child to enjoy a passage too difficult for him to read by himself;*
- *the adult to carry the child for a while, in order to ease his workload, even though he is capable of reading the passage by himself;*
- *the child to experience Chiming in once again.*

Figure 3.3	Child reading by himself with frequent alternatives – adult providing support and feedback

Child's action: reading by himself with frequent alternatives

Adult's actions:
- responding positively to alternatives by:
  - being flexible in passing over close alternatives which do not distort the meaning
  - not rushing straight in when the child pauses
  - accepting and valuing the child's alternatives
  - using the language and intonations of acceptance;
- evaluating the child's performance in order to decide:
  - whether to take over and read for the child
  - whether to select any word for focus and study.

Figure 3.4   Adult dealing with certain alternatives as focus words

Child's contribution:
- producing the alternative which reveals some good cueing knowledge.

Adult's actions:
- noticing the alternative which demonstrates some cueing knowledge;
- deciding to make that word a focus word;
- feeding back to child his own demonstrated cueing knowledge;
- supplying author's word in order to regain language flow.

Do not interrupt the flow of the text too much – keep the sense of enjoyment.

Figure 3.5   Adult making one focus word into a study word

Adult's actions:
- noticing the Cue talk potential of a focus word from:
  - some good cueing knowledge in the child's initial attempt
  - features in the word or the text offering potential for the extension of cueing knowledge;
- guiding the child to make use of those unused cues;
- protecting the child from stress if he can not yet use the cues by supplying the word and moving on.

Five sessions per week, no more than one study word per session. Maintain the confidence, enterprise and enjoyment of the Chiming in stage.

Furthermore, for some adults a positive approach to mistakes does not come easily. Some teachers may need to rethink their style of support; some parents, understandably, may need to curb their natural instincts – this is not always easy when teaching your own child.

We hope Figures 3.1 to 3.6 will prove helpful as a framework for training presentations.

The benefits offered by Cue talk are far-reaching to both child and adult. They are summarized in Figure 3.6.

Figure 3.6	Summary of the benefits of Cue talk

Cue talk allows the child to:	Cue talk allows the adult to:
reflect on his own thought processes	acquire clear evidence of the child's understanding of Broad and Fine cueing strategies
put these thought processes into words	ascertain the child's level of confidence to 'have a go' at words
receive confirmation that he is on the right lines	identify the child's immediate learning needs for that session
prepare for transfer of this learning to other situations	provide specific feedback to meet immediate need
begin to build a framework of technical vocabulary for talking about reading	build up the child's self-esteem by responding positively to his ideas
strengthen his new knowledge	increase the child's confidence by encouraging a range of alternatives

Chapter 4

Assisted reading

The child is becoming independent in his use of cues.
The adult guides his choice of cues for those words which challenge
him.

Responsibility ratios 40 : 60 to 20 : 80

Part 1 The nature of Assisted reading

CHARACTERISTICS OF ASSISTED READING

For a child to be at the stage of Assisted reading, he should know what a cue is, and should have some awareness of the following concepts:

1 There is bound to be at least one cue for any word – probably more than one.
2 Looking for cues is like going on a journey, and there may be several possible routes.
3 The 'traveller' needs to develop speed, for the benefits from contextual information are lost when fluency is impaired.

RECOGNIZING A READER AT THE ASSISTED READING STAGE

In addition to the expected understandings which we have already outlined, the reader:

• independently finds and uses appropriate cues – provided text is at an appropriate level;
• often self-corrects – and may reveal certain strategies in so doing;
• is acquainted with a range of strategies – but will need help at times to select and apply them;
• can discuss some of his strategies, indicating that he does 'own' them – but will need help to develop others.

He has graduated to a point where he can read some books by himself. For instance, he can now read independently those self-same books which he read with support at the Cue talk stage. This is not mere rote learning, for he can also manage their equivalents, books which have simple texts with short sentences, high-frequency vocabulary, and clear picture cues for less frequent vocabulary. Examples of the type of text which the reader can read independently are given in Figures 4.1 and 4.2. Figure 4.1 shows what we would expect of a reader entering into this fourth stage. Figure 4.2 illustrates what might be expected of a reader ready for Branching out.

Figure 4.1   Independent reading at the beginning of Assisted reading

He rushed to the door every morning to catch the postman. 'Oh, I'm sorry!' said Willy when the postman brought nothing for him.
   But one day a package arrived . . .

from *Willy the Wimp* by Anthony Browne

Figure 4.2   Independent reading at the end of Assisted reading

The hole the machines had dug was like the crater of a volcano. It was such an extraordinary sight that crowds of people came rushing out from the surrounding villages to have a look. They stood on the edge of the crater and stared down at Boggis and Bunce and Bean.
   'Hey, there, Boggis! What's going on?'
   'We're after a fox!'
   'You must be mad!'
   The people jeered and laughed. But this only made the three farmers more furious and more obstinate and more determined than ever not to give up until they had caught the fox.

from *Fantastic Mr Fox* by Roald Dahl

It is important to realize that the two texts in Figures 4.1 and 4.2 show what the child can read *without* support. However, the bulk of this chapter is about reading *with* support, and the quality of that support.

The following three examples give some idea of its nature. Ian, James and Sarah – snapshots of whose Assisted reading appear next – are learners whose performances typify in various ways what can be expected of readers at this stage. The snapshots also illustrate the role of the adult (Figures 4.3, 4.4 and 4.5).

Figure 4.3	Instructional reading at Assisted reading – Ian

Ian had met a word which, although in his oral vocabulary, was unfamiliar to him in its written form. He was discovering how useful the text can be when tackling such a word by reading on . . . And on . . .

The sentence was: 'His father made him a toy theatre, and his mother showed Hans Christian how to make clothing for his cardboard actors and actresses out of bright scraps left over from the dressmaking of the wealthy ladies whose washing Ann-Marie did now and then.' However, his only difficult word in this convoluted over-lengthy sentence was **theatre**.

IAN: *'His father made him a toy . . .'* [long pause]
TEACHER: What are you going to do now, Ian? [prompting Ian to verbalize his strategy]
IAN: *Read to the end of the sentence, the full stop.*
TEACHER: OK.
IAN: *'. . . and his mother showed Hans Christian how to make clothing for his cardboard actors and actresses out of bright scraps left over from the dressmaking of the wealthy ladies whose washing Ann-Marie did now and then.'* [pauses]
TEACHER: Why did he need cardboard actors and actresses? What did his dad make him?
IAN: [pauses] *Ah! he's making little figures for his theatre!*
TEACHER: Tell me how you got that word?
IAN: *Actors . . . actresses . . . and I used* **th**.

Figure 4.4	Instructional reading at Assisted reading – Sarah

Sarah, who has become confident in her predictions, is now learning to give necessary attention to cues.

She came to two sentences which read (in the original): 'The caterpillar nibbled the tender young leaves and got fatter and fatter. She was very happy.'

SARAH: *'The caterpillar nibbled the tender young leaves and got* **tummy ache**.*'* [Sarah predicted 'tummy ache' without attention to the letters.]

The teacher did not intervene, but allowed Sarah to pick up a cue from later in the text, by letting her read on.

SARAH: *'She was very happy . . .' Ah!* . . . [Sarah is prompted by this contextual cue to go back to self-correct, checking her correction against a phonic cue] *'and got fatter and fatter.'*

TEACHER: What made you change 'tummy ache'? [prompting her to verbalize her strategy]

SARAH: *Tummy ache doesn't make you happy, and anyway that's* **f-at**.

Figure 4.5   Instructional reading at Assisted reading – James

For the new word, **cardinal**, James had to rely on a wholly phonic attack as he had no prior knowledge and there were no Broad cues in the text.

His book was a reference book showing different species of insect. He had the picture, and he was able to read **beetle**, in the caption 'This beetle is a cardinal beetle.'

The term **cardinal** was completely new to him, as his intonation showed.

JAMES: *This beetle is a* **car** . . . **din** . . . **al** – cardinál? – cárdinal *beetle. 'This beetle is a cardinal beetle.'*

ASSISTED READING: THE CHILD'S TASK

The child's task over this stage is to become virtually independent in the use of cues. He must become increasingly adept in retaining and refining his Cue talk proficiency in cueing strategies, as his texts become more and more difficult.

But cueing strategy (Reading the lines) is not the only area for growth at this stage. There are two more:

- he must develop an increasing awareness of the subtleties and hidden meanings implied by authors (Between the lines);
- he should respond to what he reads with increasing insight (Beyond the lines).

ASSISTED READING: THE ADULT'S TASK

Assisted reading is, to a great extent, two people enjoying a book, requiring both adult and child to be genuinely interested in the books and what the authors are saying. The adult's close involvement with the child's understanding is necessary because most children need support to uncover what is Between the lines. Likewise, most children need adult help to extend their thinking Beyond the lines, by being persuaded to discuss their own reactions and views. Interestingly, this added attention to Between and Beyond the lines has direct impact on Reading the lines, for comprehension and appreciation heighten the reader's responsiveness to all types of cue. This triple development, then – in cueing strategies, comprehension and appreciation – comes from the adult playing an active role. It will not result from an adult passively 'Hearing reading'.

Assisted reading contrasted with 'Hearing reading'

The focus of Hearing reading has traditionally been narrow, with an overemphasis on immediate word accuracy: 'Does he get each word right?' The child is led to concentrate on each word almost in isolation, which makes comprehension difficult. It is as though the text is seen as a list of words, which must receive a mental tick before the child can move on, any unknown word being analysed on the spot. The reading can become so disjointed as to have the effect of blocking the flow of useful information coming from the text as a whole (Broad cues).

Hearing reading, then, is perhaps better described as 'Checked reading'; the adult checking up on the child's accuracy, which also checks the flow of meaning.

Assisted reading, on the other hand, seeks to make use of Broad cues, linking the flow of meaning to word attack. It encourages the child to be less concerned about the immediate analysis of an unknown word, stressing instead the need to maintain speed and utilize this fluency as a means of accessing every type of cue, Broad as well as Fine. It places greater emphasis on swift searches for meaning in the text ahead, and encourages backtracking. This encouragement to move to and fro in the text allows the reader to return to difficult words with additional, contextual, knowledge. The reader is now bringing meaning to the phonic cues. So what may seem 'a lack of rigour' – this freedom to explore the text – actually produces a more effective word attack. The goal of reading accuracy is attained – with added understanding.

The divide between Checked reading and Assisted reading is considerable. Checked reading overrelies on the individual parts. Assisted reading regards the whole as greater than just the sum of the parts. Figures 4.6 and 4.7 illustrate this.

Assisted reading: an analogy

With its emphasis on demonstration, discussion and practice, the nature of Assisted reading is well described by analogy with another field of learning.

At this stage, learning to read is like learning to ski. Once a new skier has acquired some essential skills, his instructor's role expands to include that of guide. A similar switch is required of the adult assisting the learner-reader. Hence our choice of *Assisted reading* as the label for this stage.

This is the stage when the instructor (guide) realizes that the skier has developed to a point where he actually needs some degree of challenge,

Figure 4.6	A comparison of Checked reading and Assisted reading 1

Checked reading ('Hearing reading')	Assisted reading
Interaction largely confined to word attack	Two people actively enjoying a book together
Text seen as a list of words	Text seen as a fabric of cues
Overemphasis on word accuracy	Comprehension and appreciation utilized to improve word accuracy
Reliance on the language being an easily crackable phonic code	Recognition of need for flexible cueing strategies
Unknown words analysed on the spot	Freedom to move to and fro in the text allows meaning to be brought to phonic cues
Acceptance of frequent hold-ups in the reading, which block the flow of information from the whole text	Emphasis on the need to maintain speed, using fluency to access every type of cue

while still enjoying the freedom of extended runs on easier slopes for most of the time. The instructor is as much concerned with the selection of appropriately demanding terrain as she is with skills. Can the pupil maintain and refine existing skills on more difficult slopes? Can he also cope with the introduction of new techniques on these grounds? The instructor knows that the skier will fall from time to time, but provided this is not too often, he will accept his falls as opportunities for analysis and learning. The learner is also allowed to enjoy those skills he has mastered, building his confidence by providing opportunities for him to enjoy easier ground as well.

Applying the analogy to reading, then, the good guide assists by:

- ensuring some time is spent on easy texts;
- providing some challenging books;
- focusing the learner on the forthcoming read;
- giving relevant feedback;
- linking relevant practice to feedback;
- cautioning against reverting to bad habits when tackling increasingly difficult texts;
- introducing new skills whenever feedback indicates;
- ending tuition while the learner is still enthusiastic and happy;
- leaving the learner with one specific aspect to consider between sessions;
- avoiding overtiring the learner.

Furthermore, to continue the analogy, failure to correctly match slopes and skier can produce dramatic outcomes: loss of confidence, loss of

Figure 4.7   A comparison of Checked reading and Assisted reading 2

Example 1: Strategy on meeting a word completely outside the reader's phonic experience

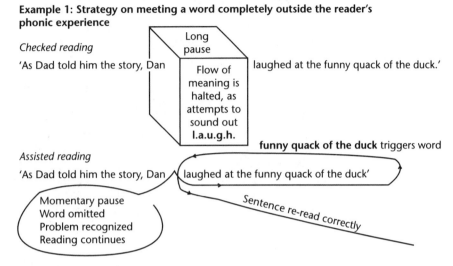

Example 2: Strategy on meeting a word containing *some* unfamiliar phonics

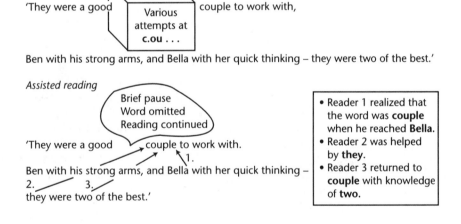

interest, reluctance to continue, even outright fear. Failure to match text and reader can produce similar outcomes.

An equation

In order for reading development to take place the challenge of unknown words is necessary, the problem-solving process being a cause of progress. This would seem to suggest a simple equation: the greater the number of problems, the greater the progress.

This is an attractive premise, but deceptively simple. In fact, it is a fallacy because it fails to recognize a key element in problem-solving, that of information-gathering. The construction of solutions relies on the pulling together of relevant information. Reduce the sources of information, and the problem-solver lacks the necessary building blocks.

However, that attractively simple equation does sit comfortably with the view of reading described earlier as Checked reading, which considers that the key to solving the problem of a word lies solely in the word itself. Given this isolated-word approach, in which the surrounding words are not seen as relevant or helpful, it would seem not to matter that a text be strewn with problem words.

And here lies the heart of a problem which has beset the teaching of reading for many years: a widespread presumption that learning to read is inevitably hard work, involving a narrow, steep, sometimes painful climb; a presumption that each day's reading will contain a few more challenges than that of the day before; a presumption of an inflexible type of support, always preoccupied with words in isolation, disregarding the ratio of unknown words to known words.

A solution

However, once a shift is made to the view that the text is a fabric of cues and the key to any problem word lies as much in its surrounding text as in itself, then the ratio of known to unknown words emerges as of central importance. And equally important is the understanding that a change in ratio requires a change in support.

So, in this chapter we shall now go on to discuss a fundamental and valuable concept: *a reader has three reading levels, and each reading level requires a different type of support.*

First, we shall give some explanation of what is meant by a reader's three levels, demonstrating why each one is important, and why a learner needs a balance of all three.

This will be followed by a discussion on how to turn this concept into practical reality, for children and parents.

Finally, we detail the close support which goes on in an Assisted reading session. This is one-to-one support at Instructional level, one of the three levels described next in Part 2.

Part 2 *The three reading levels*

MATCHING TEXT TO READER FOR DIFFERENT TUITION PURPOSES

Knowledge of how to match reader, text and tuition is central to effective support in this stage of Assisted reading.

The ratio of known to unknown words in the text is the deciding factor in determining whether the child should be:

- reading it successfully by himself;
- reading it with close support;
- listening to it being read.

Clearly, this match will be more easily made with some kind of gauge to indicate the greater or lesser extent to which a reader can cope with a particular text.

The three terms in Figure 4.8 were coined by Betts in 1957, but remain valid 40 years on, and will do so for another 40 years because they represent stages common to all learning. They deserve much greater currency in schools and homes than at present.

While we are aware that any quantifying of language is (thankfully) imprecise, we suggest nevertheless that, interpreted with common-sense, Betts's formulae are invaluable guidelines.

Figure 4.8   The three reading levels

These indicate the greater or lesser extent to which a reader can cope with a particular text.

Betts's original formula:

Independent level	Instructional level	Frustrational level
• not more than one word recognition error per 100 words • comprehension of at least 90 per cent • reading well-phrased, natural intonation • freedom from tension and anxiety	• not more than one word recognition error per 20 words • comprehension of at least 75 per cent • after silent study reads the passage in a conversational tone with proper phrasing and without tension	• errors and refusals to attempt to read difficult words are numerous, as many as 10 per cent of the running words • comprehension is less than half what is read • tension, distractibility, withdrawal from task

Probable reading capacity level

The most difficult paragraph on which the student can comprehend at least 75 per cent when it is read aloud to him; he can pronounce and use properly many of the words and language structures in the selection.

The levels have been widely reinterpreted within the following ranges:

Independent level	Instructional level	Frustration level
0–3 word recognition problems per 100 words *The child can read alone*	3–10 word recognition problems per 100 words *The level for Assisted reading*	10 or more problem words per 100 words *The child gains experience through this being read to him*

A reader at the Assisted reading stage should experience a balanced diet of all three levels.

A cautionary tale

Before we look more closely at the benefits which the learner derives from relevant experience at each of Betts's three levels, the following cautionary tale illustrates the importance of making a correct match. This is one child's laboured attempt at a Frustration level passage in which problem words occur at a rate of 13 in 100.

Roald Dahl and William

William was desperate to read Dahl's *The Twits*. Here he is tackling the part in which Mr Twit is trying to make Mrs Twit believe that she is shrinking, by sticking a tiny sliver of wood onto the bottom of her walking stick, night after night. In Figure 4.9, every underlined word is a word proving too difficult for him.

Figure 4.9	Frustration level reading at Assisted reading

This made the stick longer, but the <u>difference</u> was so small, the next morning Mrs Twit didn't <u>notice</u> it.

The <u>following</u> night, Mr Twit stuck on another <u>tiny</u> bit of wood. Every night, he crept downstairs and added an <u>extra</u> <u>tiny</u> thickness of wood to the end of the walking stick.

He did it very <u>neatly</u> so that the <u>extra</u> bits looked like a part of the old stick.

<u>Gradually</u>, but oh so <u>gradually</u>, Mrs Twit's walking stick was getting longer and longer.

Now when something is growing very slowly, it is almost <u>impossible</u> to <u>notice</u> it <u>happening</u>.

There has been a complete mismatch between what William was being expected to read for himself and what was genuinely at his Independent level.

Certainly there are children like William who, because they are motivated, want (or are expected) to tackle material which is actually too difficult. If children are constantly faced with text which is too difficult they almost cease to expect meaning – replacing some words with a mumble – and all too easily reading becomes synonymous with failure.

This is not to say that Frustration level is to be omitted from the reading diet. With the appropriate support it is a staple component. All three levels are vital, and in the following pages we explain why. (These pages may be copied for use as separate information sheets.)

Figure 4.10 **The importance of Frustration level experience (10 or more problem words per 100 words)**

This text is for listening to, only. The child should 'read it by proxy', through hearing it read to him. The child should never be asked to read at this level, either alone or in Assisted reading sessions.

Despite its forbidding label, Frustration level text is an important part of a child's reading diet. The text in question will only cause the child 'frustration' if he is being asked to read it. However, if he is allowed to experience such books by hearing them read aloud (live, recorded, or pair-read – see page 140), he should understand at least 75 per cent. He will be familiar with many of the words and language structures, yet will be acquiring new vocabulary and extending his knowledge of language. So, being read to is an essential component of a good reading diet, and should continue even when the child's reading is developing well. Teachers and many parents do continue to read books to their children, and they should be encouraged by the realization that this practice is a great deal more than cosy relaxation. It is indispensable preparation for the next developmental stage.

It is needed because:

- it provides experience of the more complex language (vocabulary and structure) necessary for reading development to continue;
- it provides essential experience of a wider range of authors, genres and registers than the learner can read for himself (this should include information text);
- it may well offer a better match with his oral language, his maturity and his interests than books at Independent and Instructional levels;
- it keeps alive his interest and enjoyment in books until he can 'Branch out'.

Frustration level, then, does have an important place. However, it is dependent on the text being read to the child, and unfortunately children sometimes misguidedly attempt to treat something at this level as though it were their Independent level. These potentially damaging mismatches sometimes go unnoticed for various reasons:

- when a child has been classed as a completely 'free reader' too early in his reading development;
- if, at any stage, a child's 'free choice' is not monitored regularly;
- or it can happen that children are tempted to read a book by having encountered it in another medium: 'I want to read this because I've seen it on TV.'

Figure 4.11	The importance of Instructional level experience (3–10 word recognition problems per 100 words)

Children should only work on this level for short periods of time, with adult support. This is Assisted reading. Unhappily, some children are expected to read nothing but this level: 'If it isn't difficult it's not doing him any good.' Such overexposure, especially if without support, leads to poor reading habits and loss of interest.

At this level the reading is reasonably fluent, although interrupted by word recognition problems, which are not always evenly spaced.

Although a child needs to be reading at Instructional level for only a small proportion of his reading week, it is a very important portion. This is the cutting edge of his new learning. The greater number of words which a child can read effortlessly are balanced against a smaller number of new and difficult words demanding efficient use of cueing tactics. So, although the sessions are comparatively short, they are intensive.

Informed support is essential, with the adult sometimes helping the child to find the right cues, and at other times more appropriately simply supplying the difficult word.

The child will need some time to prepare his reading of the text before reading it aloud with the adult.

Instructional level experience guided by an informed adult is vital because:

- it extends knowledge of cueing strategies;
- it practises known strategies on more difficult text;
- it allows the introduction of different varieties of text (genres);
- it provides satisfaction from meeting challenges;
- it allows the child to read books closer to his interest level;
- it allows the child to see he is making progress;
- it helps to develop the child's concept of reading levels.

(The 'snapshots' of Ian, James and Sarah on pages 63–4 are examples of readers working at Instructional level.)

Figure 4.12	The importance of Independent level experience (0–3 word recognition problems per 100 words)

The majority of a child's reading should be at this level, because reading should be enjoyable. This level should not be dismissed as unchallenging: 'This book's too easy for you; put it back!' The child is not in a race.

As its name implies, the child needs no support at Independent level. He needs to be reading at this level for the majority of his reading time. This is reading at which he is confident, relaxed and fluent, with (at the very most) never more than three problems in any 100 words. It is text read at first sight without any preparation, with cueing strategies being used competently and intuitively, and with almost 100 per cent comprehension. It often includes books which have become firm favourites of the child, learned by heart through having been shared countless times with a long-suffering adult. All too often this level is dismissed as 'too easy' and 'unchallenging', but we would maintain that it is vital for the child because:

- it provides the true experience of reading – i.e. he is unaware of the page;
- it makes him feel he has 'joined the literacy club';
- it puts him in control;
- it builds his self-image as a reader;
- it allows consolidation of existing skills;
- it gives him the option of successfully reading out loud;
- it permits free choice within a selected range, thereby developing his 'choosing skills';
- it allows him to read for information on selected texts;
- it builds reading stamina.

The balanced reading diet: Sam's day

Readers at this stage need to have experience of these three levels each week. We recommend ten to fifteen minutes of Assisted reading four or five times a week, with longer periods of Independent experience, interspersed with listening to Frustration level text as it is read aloud. On a typical day, for instance, Sam, Year 4, may have had the following reading experiences:

At school

His teacher read to the whole class a science text about the Beaufort Wind Scale (Frustration level), then involved them in comparing it with the poetic language of Rosetti's 'Who has seen the wind?'

He read quietly to himself for two five-minute periods, one just after morning registration, then again as the afternoon session began.

As one of a group of six, he worked with his teacher to supply some of the words deleted from a shared text at the group's Instructional level.

He went with a volunteer helper for a one-to-one Assisted reading session during his afternoon's work.

At home

As soon as he got home, his mum was able that day to find time for reading together. Today his book from school was at his Independent level, so he read it all through to her, and they had a good laugh at some of the pictures.

Mum then suggested he read it to his younger sister, because the pictures were so funny, so he got another go at reading the whole book (Independent level).

His gran came round later, and she had a new comic for him. He loved the picture stories in it (Independent level), and Gran read the full-length story to him (Frustration level).

At bedtime it was Dad's turn, and he read a book with press-button sound effects, *Hunchback of Notre-Dame*. Because it was bedtime Dad did not ask him to work too hard, so he read it for Sam, while engineering lots of opportunities for Chiming in (Instructional level).

So Sam's 'readingful' day was achieved without it being too onerous for any one adult – his teacher included. His balanced experience came from good teamwork.

While all readers need to have experience of these three levels each week, the learning needs of any one child will vary from time to time, thereby calling for a greater emphasis on one of the levels more than the others.

Figure 4.13 shows how and why the emphasis of the three levels should match the child's current needs.

Figure 4.13   Balancing the reading levels to match the child's needs

Description of child	Prescription	Purpose of prescription
The child who is getting along fine, steadily improving his repertoire of cueing strategies	4–5 Assisted reading sessions per week (Instructional level) *The other two levels provided in balance*	Instructional level reading: extends knowledge of cueing strategies; practises known strategies on more difficult text; allows the introduction of different genres; provides satisfaction from meeting challenges; allows reading of books closer to interest level; allows child to see he is making progress; helps to develop the child's concept of reading levels
The child who has been oversupported. He has been spoonfed, people reading to him at the expense of necessary Instructional work (Assisted reading)	Needs more challenge, and to develop the awareness of his own responsibility in tackling text at his Instructional level. 4–5 Assisted reading sessions per week (Instructional) *The other two levels provided in balance*	

Description of child	Prescription	Purpose of prescription
The child who has a scant awareness of story structures, and limited receptive vocabulary. He has missed out on Bookbinding, having had very little experience of books during his pre-school years	The time earmarked for Assisted reading should be mainly for the child to listen to stories being read and to discuss them. Lots of talk about the stories and the pictures A small amount of this time given to Assisted reading (Instructional) *All normal Independent reading experience also provided*	Frustration level reading: provides experience of more complex language; provides experience of a range of authors, genres and registers; offers a better match with child's (oral language), maturity and interests; keeps alive his interest and enjoyment in books
The child who has had too much experience of Checked reading, and who sees reading as something done for the benefit of the adult. He does not attempt to self-correct wrong words, as he is not attending to meaning	Plenty of Independent level reading, with the opportunity to talk about the books, and respond to them Time in Assisted reading sessions to talk Between and Beyond the lines *All normal Frustration level experience also provided*	Independent level reading provides the true experience of reading; makes the child feel he has joined the literacy club; puts him in control; builds his self-image as a reader; allows consolidation of existing skills; permits free choice with a selected range; allows reading for information on selected texts
The child who hardly ever reads without the company of an adult. He needs to learn that reading is for his own reasons, his own enjoyment	Plenty of Independent reading, to develop his reading stamina and the enjoyment of reading *The other two levels provided in balance*	
The child who is being pressured at home, through being expected to read Instructional level text as if it were Independent. He consequently has very low self-esteem	Needs to discover the pleasure of reading, at his true Independent level *The other two levels provided in balance*	

Description of child	Prescription	Purposes of prescription
The child who is being pressured at home, to read Frustration level text as though it were his Instructional level. This has produced a very low self-esteem	Confidence restored by plenty of reading at his Independent level Care taken to ensure texts at his genuine Instructional level are provided for Assisted reading *All normal Frustration level experience also provided*	Independent level reading provides all the things listed on the previous page.

FROM AWARENESS TO PRACTICE: THE TRAFFIC LIGHT SYSTEM

Pupil awareness

Figure 4.13 looks at the child's reading experience very much from the adult's point of view. However, there are several reasons why the child himself also benefits from adding an awareness of his own three levels to his 'knowledge about reading' (Kingman 1988):

- he feels in control of his own learning because he understands more about how he is learning;
- his self-esteem improves because he is not demoralized by difficult texts, for which there will be appropriate support;
- he is less likely to view reading as a 'race', because there is an overriding emphasis on gaining meaning;
- he becomes familiar with the ease and pace of real reading because he reads a great deal at Independent level;
- he realizes that the slower pace and hard work of Instructional level reading does not represent real reading because he is so familiar with the ease and pace of Independent level reading;
- he accepts the slower pace and hard work of Instructional level reading because he sees it as a 'master class' experience;
- he can recognize his own improvement because books which were Instructional level become Independent level;
- he is less anxious because his expectations, and his parents' expectations, are realistically informed by knowledge of the levels;
- he chooses books sensibly because he has clear purposes and strategies for selection;
- his appreciation of cueing strategies is strengthened because he realizes that the majority of known words on a page can help him bring meaning to the analysis of the minority of difficult words.

A traffic light system

This concept – that each learner has his own individual levels of competence – has to be turned into something children actually use in everyday practice. A 'traffic light system' can achieve this.

Introducing the concept

The bicycle poster shown in Figure 4.14 can provide a focus for a group or individual to classify personal recent reading under its three headings, introduced by the teacher's own recent reading experiences.

Signalling the level of each book as it is used

Key to the functioning of the system are the traffic light bookmarks which repeat the captions of the bicycle poster (Figure 4.14). These are shown in Figure 4.15.

Figure 4.14   The three reading levels illustrated

Independent level	Instructional level	Frustration level
I could keep going all day	*Help me over difficulties*	*Can't go on. Please help me*
I can read this on my own	I can read this with help	I can't read this. Please read it for me

Figure 4.15   Traffic light bookmarks

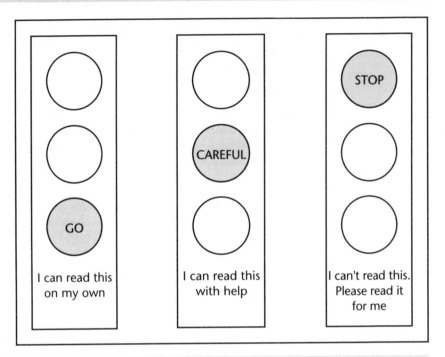

Each classroom needs a plentiful supply of these bookmarks, in each of the three colours, stored so as to be easily accessible to the children. The appropriate card is inserted into any book that is either going home or going to a supporting adult in the school. It serves as a signal to both child and adult as to how the book should be attempted, and provides a framework to enable the child to articulate his own understanding of the three levels.

(The green traffic light: 'I can read this on my own' may mean, as it did for Tracy, 'I like to curl up in a corner and read this to myself.' Or it may mean what Abigail meant, 'I like to read this to my gran to show I can do it.' Both interpretations are equally valid.)

Maintaining the system

It is important to ensure that the system remains a priority. The following suggestions help to maintain interest and awareness:

- train children to take passages of 100 words and to count the number of difficult words;
- train them to use that information when matching bookmark to book;
- display a copy of the bicycle poster in book corners and the library;
- keep a supply of bookmarks in the classroom to counter the inevitable losses; children can colour their own or stick on coloured spots;

- make a regular feature of talking to children about their choice of bookmark for a specific book;
- record colour of bookmark beside book title on reading records – both the home–school reading card and the within-school records;
- monitor parents' comments on home–school records to make sure the traffic light instructions continue to be useful to them;
- make sure the system retains a high profile with parents.

COMMUNICATING THE THREE READING LEVELS TO PARENTS

It is crucially important that parents be advised of the appropriate support for any books their child brings home, and 'traffic lights', like their real-life counterparts, help to ensure children's safety. Traffic light bookmarks serve as regular practical reminders of the need to match support style to book level. Each book going home in the typical reading bag or plastic wallet should carry with it this simple clear signal as to the parents' reading role with that book.

Over the course of a week a child should experience books at his three levels. In order to achieve this, schools will need to think of books as being of two types. Type A are those books which schools variously describe as reading books, scheme books or class readers. These should go home bearing a green traffic light. They will have been selected for the child by the teacher to ensure an enjoyable and successful reading experience:

- they may be books quite new to the child but known to be at his Independent level, perhaps taken from the core scheme or a parallel scheme;
- they may be books recently converted to the child's Independent level through recent Instructional level work. For example, on Friday Ross takes home the book he has worked on all week in daily sessions in class.

Type B books are books which the child has selected for himself. Schools variously describe these as sharing books, choosing books, own choice books, library books or free readers. They go home with the appropriate traffic light bookmark: red, orange or green. As the purpose of Type B books is to increase and maintain the child's awareness of the wealth of reading outside scheme books, care must be taken to ensure that his choices retain a balance of all three levels. It is equally important for him to listen to demanding language, to romp through easy text with delight and to rehearse – with support – previously learned cueing strategies.

For parents sometimes the distinction between the types of support can become blurred, especially as memories of any reading meeting fade. Then the child is required, with detrimental consequences, to read aloud Frustration and Instructional level books as though they were at his Independent level. And, adding further insult to injury, he may not be left alone to read Independent level books which he could well enjoy all by himself.

So, the traffic light bookmarks which we show in Figure 4.15 are useful devices to prevent any misunderstandings, serving to preserve in the adult's mind the notion that there are different types of support. They provide informative guidance on the three levels, any or all of which may be in the reading bag on any one night. Of course, they are only of real use if the system has been explained to the adults at a reading meeting (see Chapter 6), or on a one-to-one basis.

If the parents have attended a meeting, the information can go home in the form of a 'master-card' to serve as a constant reminder. Figure 4.16 provides templates for just such a fold-over, take-home leaflet.

But even where parents have not been able to attend, this card can still act as a guide. The fact that it is in card form gives it a greater chance of being kept safe – behind the clock, stuck to the fridge – and used constantly. It presents its information briefly, and, in a busy household, is easily recognizable from its traffic light design. Also, perhaps it is more appealing than a plain list of dos and don'ts.

The two inside pages are self-explanatory, but the back of the card deals with a more complex type of support for Instructional level. This is Assisted reading, and it needs a degree of training – its effectiveness is dependent upon having had much more detailed explanation and instruction than a card summary can supply. We believe that the pick-and-mix suggestions which we give will not do any actual harm if used without background information. But we do strongly suggest that without the added understanding which a meeting can give, they will not be as effective.

Part 3 Ingredients of an Assisted reading session

A child at the Assisted reading stage would benefit from as many as four or five sessions of Instructional level reading in a week. Realistically, a school should endeavour to provide two or three.

In a session, adult and child will read about 500 words. From this 500 or so, one passage of about 100 words will be a 'study-passage'. For every study-passage there will need to be a run-in of another 100 words or so, and the remaining 300 will be covered with significant adult support at greater speed in order to move the child on through the story. This is done so that – even at this stage where close attention is given to the mechanics of cueing – there is the constant message that reading is about meaning and satisfaction.

In Assisted reading sessions there will be times when:

- the adult reminds the child of the purposes of Assisted reading;
- the adult reads parts of the text *to* the child;
- the adult reads parts of the text *with* the child;
- the adult ensures the child is 'tuned in';
- the child silently pre-reads the study-passage before reading it aloud;

Figure 4.16   Help your child to read the traffic light way: a take-home leaflet

FOLD

Panel 4

Never spend more than 5 minutes on Assisted Reading

Assisted reading

When your child meets a problem word, Pick and Mix what to say:

- 'Any clues in the picture?'
- 'Can you think of any words that might fit'
- 'Now look again at the word on the page. From it's letters, does it match one of your words?'
- 'Read up to that word again.'
- 'Keep going. Read past it. Look for clues.'
- 'Read up to that word again, and just say its beginning.'
- 'Read up to it, say its beginning, and read on past it.'

If all this clue-searching is getting nowhere, just tell your child the word

4

Panel 1

Help your child to read

STOP

CAREFUL

GO

The traffic-light way

1

Panel 2

STOP

CAREFUL

GO

The Red light
Stop
Do not let your child read this book alone. Have fun as _you_ read it aloud

STOP

CAREFUL

GO

The Green light
Go, Go, Go
Your child can read this book alone

2

Panel 3

STOP

CAREFUL

GO

The Orange light
Careful!
Your child needs help to read this book

Gently say _every_ word which your child can't read. Say it so quickly and smoothly that the reading just flows.

There is also ASSISTED READING. Please do not attempt this unless you have had it explained to you by the school

3

- the adult and child discuss the study-passage before the child reads it aloud;
- the child reads the study-passage aloud, while the adult supports his use of a full range of cues on problem words, and adult and child comment about content;
- the adult closes the session on a positive note.

In the following pages we describe each of these components in more detail. Although circumstances will determine the order in which they occur in the session, they all have a valuable part to play in drawing together Broad and Fine cues, and promoting their effective use.

THE ADULT REMINDS THE CHILD OF THE PURPOSES OF ASSISTED READING

- The adult puts the child at ease, by letting him know how long the session will last, and that it will not consist solely of his hard work on the study passage.

'Right, John! Let's work on this now for 15 minutes. You'll have to work hard for about ten minutes of that, and then I promise I'll read the rest of the chapter for you, so we'll really get on with the story.'

- Revision of his cueing knowledge builds the child's confidence through reminding him that he has the tools to do the job.

'Just remind me now of all the different things you're going to do when you come to a hard word. Remember how we ran through them last time.'

- The pupil should be able to list some cueing tactics, and the adult accepts these as indication of a developing understanding.

'Brilliant! You've remembered – one, to use all the words around the new word; two, to use the pictures; three, to think about what the author means; four, to build just the first bit of the word.
    'Good. Now remember, you're going to have to think about all those things even when it gets really tricky. So don't panic . . . don't give up . . . you can do it . . .'

Such reminders are similar to a ski instructor's advice on not abandoning useful techniques when under pressure (see page 66).

- If, as can happen, the child is only allowed to progress through the book one study-passage at a time it takes far too long, is de-motivating, unrewarding and baffling – counter to the desired effect of enjoyment and increased knowledge.

'And when we've read this bit you'll be able to take it home with a red bookmark, and get someone to read it to the end of the chapter. Then you won't have to wait till next week to find out if they escape!'

THE ADULT READS PART OF THE TEXT *TO* THE CHILD

There are various reasons for this, the first one being the benefit mentioned above, of getting the child swiftly through the story. Other reasons are:

- Reading the paragraph just before a study-passage can tune in both adult and child to the author's voice and to the immediate subject matter.
- Reading sizeable chunks not only helps the child through the book but also provides a necessary model of proficient reading.
- If the child has had to battle with a study-passage, he needs the adult to re-read it for him, drawing it all together, and putting it back in the author's voice.

THE ADULT READS PARTS OF THE TEXT *WITH* THE CHILD

This is done by various means. It may be that adult and child read alternate paragraphs, or alternate characters in a conversation. Or it may be that they read short sections simultaneously (see page 140 for a more detailed account of Paired reading).

These activities serve the same purposes as the adult reading to the child:

- they serve as a model;
- they help the child through the book;
- they vary the ways of re-reading the study-passage.

TUNING IN

Tuning in is a process of drawing the child into the right mind-set for a book. Its importance is often underestimated – often overlooked altogether. Yet it can make all the difference between a successful read and a struggling read, by ensuring that the child has the background knowledge fundamental to the book.

This necessary background knowledge is almost alarmingly wide, including:

- what kind of book it is (genre);
- the author's voice (register);

- the setting of the book;
- its structure;
- its theme;
- its vocabulary.

Tuning in aims to develop, among other things, the awareness of:

- historical attitudes and customs (for example *Eagle of The Ninth* or *Noggin the Nog*);
- geographical locations (for example *Little House on the Prairie* and *The Snow Village* in Oxford Reading Tree);
- conventions of speech (for example *The Prince and the Pauper*, and many, many fairy tales);
- literary cross-references (for example nursery rhymes in *The Jolly Postman*, and traditional tales of suitors in *Princess Smarty Pants*);
- exchanges between books and electronic media (for example between *Wind in the Willows* and natural science documentaries on film);
- differences between books and their filmed and cartooned versions.

A system for tuning in

Clearly, those children with limited experience of books and of life will be at a disadvantage, and so for them especially, and the rest, a system providing some measure of this background information will be of benefit.

This system should be part of a whole-school policy which requires children to be trained in self-help routines and provided with some recorded help. Then children can experience a degree of tuning in when first picking up a book, releasing some of the precious one-to-one time needed for other aspects of Assisted reading.

However, some help has to be on the spot, without previous planning, because often the needs of the child become apparent only at the point of reading.

Tuning in can be done in three different ways: self-help routines, recorded help, and one-to-one support.

Self-help

- child looks through the pictures;
- child reads the blurb.

Although children often use the cover illustration to tune in, if left to their own devices they do not make best use of what help is provided by other features. For example, without training they are not always aware of the full value of pictures and of the blurb, nor of the way these suggest how to approach the book (for instance: is it thrilling? is it funny?). They need to be trained to become aware of how pictures and blurb suggest some of the action yet leave room for personal prediction.

By using these sources, it is possible for children to begin to fill in much more of the Broad cue area for themselves, triggering whatever bank of knowledge and vocabulary they have to bring to the text.

Recorded help, using tape, Language Master or card

Figure 4.17 summarizes the ways in which some vital background information can be supplied by the school in recorded form.

- If the gist of the story or any necessary background information is put on cassette, the tape need only be brief, perhaps about three minutes: for instance, basic facts about what sheepdogs do, in order to understand *The Sheep Pig*; the significance of white feathers in World War I to understand *The Three Feathers*; or pointers to help the child realize when an author is using humour, sarcasm or irony.

  Similar information can be printed on card for the child to read, or perhaps have read for him. This will necessarily be more concise than the tape. The tape or card should be stored together with the book in a plastic wallet.
- The key vocabulary and phrases of a book can be presented as a glossary. This should be in print rather than on tape, because the visual image of the word is needed, and pictures are helpful. It can be on card stored in a plastic wallet with the book, or alternatively it can be on paper pasted inside the book's cover.

  Even more effective is the use of the Language Master, which transforms a glossary into a talking glossary. It is a recorder/player using short segments of tape mounted on cards which are run through the machine one at a time. Each blank Language Master card carries a strip of recording tape several seconds long, with enough space for a written message plus an illustration. The Language Master is a greatly underused resource, and there is at least one already in place in most schools. With only a little ingenuity it can be put to a wide variety of uses.

Figure 4.17   Recorded help for 'tuning in'

	Cassette	Card	Language Master
Gist of story and/or background information	✓	✓	
Key vocabulary and phrases			✓
Questions before reading	✓	✓	✓

- A question relating to the content can be given to the child before he begins the book. This encourages the child to engage more closely with what he is reading, developing that level of questioning and thought which is the hallmark of a mature reader. It should not be a fact-finding question, but something to make the child think critically about characters or events, to lead him to see the point of the tale, to understand the craft of the writer, or appreciate the collaboration of writer and illustrator. For instance *Diary of a Killer Cat*, by Ann Fine: 'The writer writes this story as though she is a cat. Do you think she likes cats?'; or *The Lighthousekeeper's Lunch* by Rhonda and David Armitage: 'The pictures tell us extra things about the story. Can you spot them?'

Initially the child will need some support in the one-to-one time to carry out these suggestions for self-help and recorded help, but they soon become activities which take place outside that time.

It does take some time and effort to develop the resources, but when a school spreads the labour it is not too onerous. For example, if each teacher in the school prepares the background resources for two books per term, then over time a useful bank of material will accumulate.

One-to-one and group help

When the child is beginning a new book, these discussions about what the child has derived from his tuning in, whether self-help or recorded, will include some of the following:

- informing or reminding the child about the author, and the illustrator;
- pointing out where authors have illustrated their own books;
- commenting on the dedication;
- discussing the front cover;
- reading and commenting on the blurb;
- linking the book to any TV or film version;
- enquiring whether the child has any previous knowledge, pointing out that this need not necessarily have come from print: 'Your dad keeps pigeons, doesn't he?';
- weaving forthcoming vocabulary into the discussion: 'Have you come across the *Norman Invasion* before? The King who invaded was called William the *Conqueror*' (This may avoid the alternative provided by one reader: William the Conductor!);
- reminding the child of the genre: 'What other ghost stories have you read, or heard, or seen?';
- discussing expectations of vocabulary: 'What words would *you* use if you were writing about haunted houses?' Sometimes this could involve drawing up a word web, as shown in Figure 4.18.

When a child is part-way through a book, the adult draws the child into discussion on the story so far, perhaps asking for views on what have been the 'best bits', and together they predict outcomes. From this discussion she will be able to assess whether more tuning in is needed.

Figure 4.18   A word web for 'tuning in'

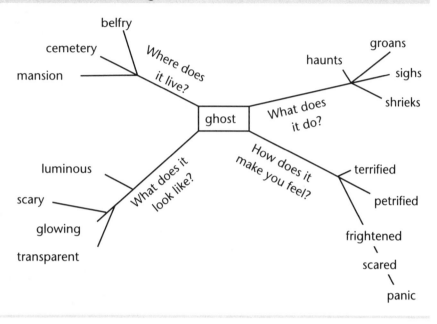

She will evaluate how much the child has genuinely comprehended, and whether he is motivated to continue.

'I don't like this one'

This question of motivation brings us to the common problem of what to do when a child loses interest and is reluctant to finish a book. There is no single simple answer, and certainly a solution will not be found under an inflexible regime which insists that every book be finished. Each case is different, and finding the individual prescription will involve asking two key questions:

- Are child and book matched correctly?
- Are adult assumptions getting in the way?

In checking the match of child and book, 'Is it too hard for him?' seems an obvious question. But perhaps a better line of questioning is:

- Is it simply the sheer length of the book, or its subject matter?
- What is the level of this book for this child? (i.e. red/Frustration level; orange/Instructional level; green/Independent level)
- Is the support properly matched to that level?

The answers to all these questions will shape the necessary changes.
However, adult assumptions may stand in the way of these changes. In Figure 4.19 we examine some representative comments and the areas of conflict which they reflect.

Figure 4.19   'I don't like this one'

Adult comment	Hidden assumption	Conflict
You've got to learn in life to finish what you've started	This adult is using the reading lesson as a lesson in life. Reading is not the central issue	On the one hand, there is a real need for children to develop 'stickability' *On the other hand they need to gain satisfaction from their reading*
You'll finish that because I've told you to	This adult's concern is obedience. Again, reading is not the central issue	
This is your reading book. You've *got* to read all of it	This adult assumes there is some special power in the 'scheme' book as the sole provider of knowledge about reading, each book an unmissable step. She has not appreciated the nature of the cueing system, nor how cueing strategies may be developed on many different kinds of material	The narrowness of schemes is an advantage for some children for some of the time, while they are building up skills and confidence, because schemes provide consistency of style, setting and vocabulary. *But there is also a danger that adults' overreliance on scheme books prevents children from accessing wider experience*
I want you to read this. It's a classic. It'll do you good	This adult assumes there is a fixed body of classic works, perhaps without having actually analysed what constitutes 'classic'	Certainly children have a right to their tastes. *However, if they are to develop the informed choices expected of mature readers, adults have a responsibility to guide them towards a wide range of genres*
All you ever read are books about football. It's time you read something different	This adult is denying the developing reader the same freedom of choice enjoyed by mature readers	
It's got to be hard or you'll never learn. You're not trying	The adult assumes not only that learning to read is inevitably hard but also that the one-to-one sessions are examinations	Learning to read requires engagement with some tough problem-solving. *But that should not be the sum total of the experience. The overall impression should be of success and enjoyment*

It is tempting to dismiss the comments and assumptions of Figure 4.19 as entrenched attitudes loaded with negative messages from the adult's own past. However, within each there is a justifiable principle which should be recognized, respected and accommodated. A practical resolution must be found with which both parties can feel satisfied. Negotiation must therefore take place, and once both adults and children realize what options are on offer, a compromise is possible. This is the only way to an improvement in atmosphere – which in turn is essential to the overall aim of more books being read.

The options which follow help to avoid any unproductive battle of wills, and the resentment which comes from loss of face.

The option of sticking with the same book but negotiating the type of support

A book may be completed by adopting various support methods:

* *Switching the load:* switching from an orange to a red traffic light marker. This acknowledges that a book at Frustration level was being attempted as if it were at the child's Instructional level. The adult now takes over the responsibility for the reading, which offers the child all those benefits of Frustration level experience which we described on page 71. Paired reading, another useful technique here, is described in detail on page 140.
* *Sharing the load:* sharing the reading of the book. This makes it possible to get through more books more quickly. It can be on a basis of, say, 12 pages read by the adult to three pages read by the child, or as we described earlier (page 83), turn and turn about (assuming the book is *not* Frustration level).
* *Reducing the load:* reducing the amount of reading by permitting the reader to skip from one pre-selected passage to another. This type of support demands that the adult know the book sufficiently well to be able to select a suitable route through the book, providing summaries of the skipped passages. Commercially produced taped versions, even videos, may sometimes supply the missing sections. Reducing the load is useful as a way of supporting slower readers so that they can take part in any class or group work based on a shared book.
* *Supporting the load:* Assisted reading. The reader's reluctance may stem from being unsure about his use of cueing tactics. It could be, in fact, that he is not in need of any fundamental change of support, but only in need of basic Assisted reading, effectively delivered. The detail of these supportive actions follows on pages 92–107.

The option of changing the book

While this option does require the adult to relinquish some control, and to accept that the responsibility for selection may, through discussion, be shared, it is a concession which usually results in improved reader commitment.

It is necessary but worthwhile to spend some time exploring with the child his likes and dislikes, while remaining open-minded about transferring to non-fiction, non-school material, short stories, joke books, poems, etc.

THE CHILD SILENTLY PRE-READS THE STUDY-PASSAGE BEFORE READING IT ALOUD

This pre-reading component of the session should reflect a whole-school policy of never asking a child to read aloud anything which he has not had time to prepare (before the stage of Branching out).

This pre-reading may take place during the session, or beforehand to save time in the session itself:

'OK, Marty. I want you to read pages six and seven, – it's about 100 words, isn't it? – and that's your orange marker in there, so we know there will be some words that are hard for you. But keep going . . . read it all through and don't stop when you come to a difficult word. Be ready to tell me what it's all about, and show me which words were hard for you.'

Being allowed to prepare a passage before reading it out loud to an adult should not be a luxury. It should be routine for all developing readers, as it promotes the habit of reading an entire passage at a reasonable speed, thereby gaining as much meaning as possible from the known words. It confirms for the child that he can return to make sense of problem words by using all the extra information he has gleaned from the rest.

In addition, such regular experience of completing a passage, persisting through difficulties, builds both confidence and stamina.

On occasions it may be useful to ask the child to highlight his problem words on an acetate overlay or a prepared photocopy of the page. This will offer him graphic demonstration of the much higher proportion of known words to unknown, a welcome focus on the positive – for child or parent. Moreover, the child himself can clearly see the position of his problem words in relation to their surrounding bed of known words, including the extra difficulty of problem words clustering together.

This technique of pre-reading the passage offers him the chance to decide his cueing tactics, and provides the framework for him to explain his working-out, as was expected of him in Cue talk.

ADULT AND CHILD DISCUSS HIS PRE-READING OF THE STUDY-PASSAGE BEFORE HE READS IT ALOUD

'Right, Pat. You've read the passage to yourself. Now give me some idea of what you've found out about the children's plans for escaping.'

In asking for a summary first, the adult is highlighting for the child the fact that he has understood a great deal, despite meeting some problem words.

'OK, here's a word you don't know yet. Well, let's think what the author could have used.'

The adult asks the child what alternatives he was able to think of for those words he could not read. This is the point at which she asks him to explain his working-out, noting whether he has sufficiently comprehended the words he can read to generate meaning for words he cannot, and noting what use he is making of phonic information. She should be mentally planning which words they will need to work on in detail in the course of the read, and preparing to supply the rest. She will be looking for the number of words manageable within the time limit. Ideally they will be words for which the child has a reasonable alternative, and words which represent useful phonics, reusable through analogy. (For example, if he can read **work** and **word**, by analogy he should be able to read '**wor**ld's **wor**st **wor**m'.) Where a number of problem words cluster together, she may decide to supply one or more, which should help unlock the rest.

TEACHER: So, Pat, you've told me one of them gets away by plane. Why do you say that?
CHILD: *'Cos it says 'he flew'* . . . [Text reads: 'He flew into a rage']

Continuing to discuss the child's understanding of the passage as a whole, the adult might need to talk about any obvious misunderstanding.

THE CHILD READS THE STUDY-PASSAGES ALOUD WHILE THE ADULT SUPPORTS HIM

This is such a vital section, we have dedicated Part 4 of this chapter to the detail of its supportive actions (page 92).

THE ADULT CLOSES THE SESSION ON A POSITIVE NOTE

Praise is always productive, and global comments such as 'Well done!' or 'Great!' are all useful. But the most productive praise focuses on some specific action. For instance:

• 'I loved the way you read on, there.'
• 'You've really got the hang of saying the word **something**, in place of the word you don't know.'
• 'Those were two super alternatives you came up with there.'

- 'Good for you, changing lă ... to lā.... *You cottoned on really quickly.'
- 'Great! You've read on through *four* sentences to search out that clue.'
- 'I liked the way you went back to the beginning of the sentence there, to have another run at it.'
- 'Well done! You've read 38 out of the 41 words in that paragraph.' (Using the actual number provides the child with hard evidence of his success.)
- 'I'm impressed. Look at some of the words you did read. You wouldn't have read those six months ago.'
- 'You've read all the words correctly, but it's still not making sense. It's the book's fault, not yours. [Text is laid-out in two lines: 'When he went up // high the sky became yellow.'] "High the sky!" – it splits the sentence in the wrong place [points to **up**]. Let me write it all on one line, then you'll get it': When he went up high, the sky became yellow.

Part 4 Ten supportive actions for a problem word

When the child reads his prepared study passage aloud, that is the key time in an Assisted reading session for close attention to the refinement and consolidation of cueing strategies.

In our three previous stages one of the adult's main aims has been to preserve the flow of meaning. By contrast, here for the first time we have a situation in which the adult actually capitalizes on those moments when the reader pauses for help, using them for teaching purposes.

So next we will describe a number of episodes illustrating ten supportive actions through which the adult consolidates and extends the child's knowledge of cueing tactics.

The episodes share the following common characteristics:

- In every episode, the reader considers possibilities for a problem word, in many instances generating a short list of possible words from which a final choice is made.
- Because reading involves making use of both phonic and meaning information, so each supportive action inevitably draws on more than one cueing tactic. These tactics will always come from each of the two categories, Fine and Broad, and the reader's strategy must be to balance them, juggling evidence from each.
- Eventually there is a moment when the light dawns as some clinching evidence clicks the word into place, and the reader maps it onto the printed word before him.
- Throughout, the adult is either:
  - demonstrating strategies for the reader or
  - supporting strategies initiated by the reader.

*A macron, ¯, is used to indicate short vowel phonemes as in cat, pen, pig, box, cup. A breve, ˘, is used to indicate the long vowel phonemes as in rain, meet, kite, bowl, truth.

- Phonic instruction is there at the heart of the reading, supplied at the point of real need, allowing it to complement other information.
- Reference is often made to other phonic instruction outside the Assisted reading session, instruction which has already taken place or will take place as a follow-up.

The ten supportive actions may be thought of under the following headings. (This list is intended as a menu, not a priority order, nor a teaching order.)

1 Thumb it.
2 Block it.
3 Hint at it.
4 Take another run at it.
5 Jump over it.
6 Re-bed it.
7 Ask about it.
8 Run up and sample it.
9 Help to build it.
10 Wait and see.

1 THUMB IT

Place your thumb over the problem word, from above the line, so that your hand does not obscure the following text. Re-read the whole sentence saying the word **something** in place of the missing word.

TEXT: Men were hard at work **busy** fixing doors and roofs.
LIN: *'Men were hard at work . . .'* [pause] *. . . ummmmm . . .*
TEACHER: Keep going.
LIN: *'. . . fixing doors and roofs'*
TEACHER: [not saying anything, points back to **busy**]
LIN: **bŭ . . . bŭ . . .**
TEACHER: [places thumb over word from above the line, leaving discussion of the unusual sound of **u** for later, in order to maintain the flow of meaning] Just think what the word might be, look at what's going on [indicating picture]. 'Men were hard at work – something – fixing doors and roofs.' [repeats] 'Men were hard at work – something – fixing doors and roofs.'
LIN: *. . . busy!* *'busy fixing doors and roofs.'* [suddenly doubtful] *Busy? It looks more like bus.*
TEACHER: Yes. **Busy** *is* a funny word. We'll talk about it at the end.

Covering the problem word with a thumb prevents the reader from viewing it as a real physical barrier. It shifts the attention from one individual word to the text surrounding that word. When repeating the sentence, it is important to use another word (perhaps **something**) in place of the problem word, because the substitution then remains language.

This works better than a non-verbal signal such as tapping the table or just leaving a gap. As language, it can be spoken keeping the same intonation as the original word. This is particularly important when the word is an adjective or an adverb – the most dispensable parts of the sentence.

The adult may have to repeat the sentence more than once, restoring fluency and expression, before the reader can supply the word.

In this particular episode, Lin's first suggestion happened to be correct. Often, however, an alternative to the author's word is given. Lin could have given **building**, or **quickly**, for example. If that had been the case, the teacher would have re-read the sentence once again, using an alternative offered: 'Men were hard at work, **building** fixing doors and roofs'; 'Men were hard at work, **quickly** fixing doors and roofs.'

Both **building** and **quickly** would be praised as the teacher reflected back to the child those cues he had sensibly used. Yet at the same time, the fault in his cueing would be identified.

'Good, I can see you were remembering the letters at the beginning of the word, and certainly they are hard at work building, but it doesn't fit with the next bit, does it . . . "building fixing doors and roofs" . . . it doesn't sound right'; or

'Good. You've found a word that makes sense, and fits into the sentence nicely. Now let's look back at the word to check if it really is **quickly**, and see if we have to do more thinking.'

Only those alternatives which match syntactically (in this sentence **quickly**, and not **building**) are taken back to the page for closer visual matching.

Note that a syntactical mismatch needs no more detailed discussion than 'it doesn't fit . . . it doesn't sound right', working via the child's experience of oral language.

2 BLOCK IT

Take the book away from the child and read him the sentence minus its problem word.

TEXT: We'll look around and then **decide** where you can sleep.
TONY: *'We'll look around and then . . .'* [pause] **d . . . ĕ . . . k . . .**
TEACHER: [noticing that there are strong context cues coming up next, and not wanting to halt the reading at this point for the necessary discussion about soft **c**] We won't try building that one just now.
TONY: **dĕk . . .**
TEACHER: [turns book over] Now forget about the letters for the moment. I'll read the sentence to you. You just have a listen. 'We'll look around and then – something – where you can sleep.' [repeats] 'We'll look around and then – something – where you can sleep.'

TONY: *Is it* **see***?*

TEACHER: Brilliant! . . . you're on the right track. That's what the author means, but it's not actually **see**. Think of another word that the author could have used. 'We'll look around and then – something – where you can sleep.'

TONY: [puzzled tone] **Decide**?

TEACHER: Yes, it is! Excellent. [turns book back] Are you thinking that should be an **s** in there? [pointing to **decide**] Do you remember when **c** has an **i** after it, it says **s**? Remind me before you go that we need to put this word on the 'cinema' page in your word book.

By taking the book away and saying the sentence, more than once if necessary, the task is changed from one of visual decoding to one of listening to oral language – an area in which a child has more strengths. Children can often be seen to look away, or look up, perhaps with eyes half shut, as their concentration shifts to the meaning and away from the problematical print. Frequently the right word will come to mind. It may well take several re-readings, varying the intonations, to find the flow-of-language prompt that works for that child.

After that, the reader returns to the print, and checks his word against its phonics.

3 HINT AT IT

Give a brief reminder of the problem word's wider setting.

TEXT: Mind you, if our **enemies** had been any good they would have finished us off straight away.

STEVIE: *'Mind you, if our en . . . en . . .'* [pause]

TEACHER: They're fighting, remember.

STEVIE: . . . *enemies*! . . . *yes '. . . enemies had been any good . . .'* [and he continues to read on correctly]

The task of Assisted reading is essentially one of balancing the use of cues, described on the two sides of the Positive Cueing Observation Sheet (see page 17). Children can become too focused on a problem word, virtually hypnotized by it. A nudge to remind them of the Broader help available is often all that is required. In this example the Broader cue has been supplied to the reader at the very point of word-building. This helps him perform that necessary juggling act of holding meaning in his mind while using phonic information to make a match with the printed word in front of him. Stevie repeats the word once, perhaps considering its sounds relative to the word he can see. This moment when the reader 'maps' the meaning onto the printed word happens in every one of our examples, after which the reader can carry on, sure of the match.

4 TAKE ANOTHER RUN AT IT

Re-read only as far as the problem word, usually from the beginning of the sentence, using a natural pace and intonation.

Example 1 Preceding words provide key information

TEXT: Each time Peter rubbed the puppy dry with a **towel** beside the fire.
MAX: *'Each time Peter rubbed the puppy dry with a . . .'* [pause]
TEACHER: 'Each time Peter *rubbed* the puppy dry with aaaa . . .'? [stressing **rubbed**; holding a rising, questioning note, stopping before **towel**]
MAX: **Towel!** *I was thinking that said* **two**, *but it didn't make sense.*
TEACHER: Yes, I can see why you thought that – the same letters are in there – but I'm glad you realized it didn't make sense.

Perhaps if, as part of a gap-reading activity, there had been a blank space in place of the word **towel, two** would never have entered into Max's thinking. But here, his attention had been captured by the look of the word, momentarily pushing out the sense.

In addition to retaining Max's confidence, the teacher's comments verbalized his working out for him, and confirmed his positive tactics:

- he was trying to use the first part of the word as a phonic prompt;
- he was running a check against the sense;
- he refrained from saying **two** because of the weight of meaning he had already gathered.

Example 2 Problem word is part of a common word-string

TEXT: It's round here somewhere, but I don't know **where**.
LEE: [reading at a word-by-word plodding pace] *'It's. round. here. somewhere. but. I. don't. know . . .'* [pause]
TEACHER: [much more quickly and with conversational intonation] 'It's round here somewhere, but I don't knooooow . . .'? [her voice rises questioningly on **know**, and she lengthens the word, to hold it. She repeats] 'It's round here somewhere, but I don't knooooow . . .'?
LEE: **Where!** [and he carries on reading the next sentence]
TEACHER: Good [whispering, hardly interrupting Lee's reading]

Because the teacher's main aim was to sustain fluency, she chose to avoid any disruptive comment. Instead she used a supportive action which is especially useful when the problem word is not a colourful noun or verb, nor a descriptive adjective or adverb, but is one of those colourless words which are the 'mortar' of language, holding together the more depictable 'bricks'. The teacher's speedy natural delivery revived Lee's own oral language memory so that he could do what is often done in conversation – finish someone else's sentence. It enabled him to anticipate **where** from a common word-string. His disjointed read was pulled back together into one unit of thought.

Note that Lee was able to read **where** in **somewhere** because it had its own in-built run-up. (The **some** . . . prompted it.) The second **where** in the sentence was removed from context by Lee's slow pace, due to a poor visual recall of basic sight vocabulary. Moreover, the run-up was composed of nothing but basic sight-vocabulary words, for which there is no colourful meaning.

The word could have been **why,** or it could have been **what**, but it seems probable that Lee ran a check against the print, as well as using the oral prompt.

5 JUMP OVER IT

Re-read the whole sentence with good intonation and at a natural pace, supplying the word **something** in place of the problem word.

Re-reading the whole sentence in this manner allows a search ahead for some useful information which has a bearing on the problem word.

TEXT: They hid in the barn and the **deafening** noise of the machine made them unable to hear anything.

AHMED: *'They hid in the barn and the dee . . .'* [pause]

TEACHER: [reading on past the problem word in order to help Ahmed realize that **deafening** and **noise** are connected, and that 'unable to hear anything' gives a strong cue, virtually a definition for **deafening**] 'They hid in the barn and the – something – noise made them unable to hear anything.' [repeats] 'They hid in the barn and the – something – noise made them unable to hear anything.'

AHMED: *Loud noise?* [Ahmed has cleverly narrowed his options by suggesting **loud**]

TEACHER: Great idea! That's the meaning. It certainly is a word telling us something about the noise. But look at the word [pointing to **deafening**]. What does **loud** begin with?

AHMED: *Oh, l, and that's a* d . . . d.ee . . . [pause, thinking] dě . . . *Is it* **deaf***?*

TEACHER: We're getting there! Excellent. Now, the word on the page has three syllables. **Deaf** has only one syllable. [reads again] 'They hid in the barn and the deaf-something noise of the machine . . .'

AHMED: **Deafening***!*

[The teacher makes a note to look at ěa words later.]

At the end of the session the teacher reminded Ahmed of the strategy he had used to get **deafening**.

Ahmed was making the most effective use of phonics by linking them to the information gathered from the available context, while adding new phonic knowledge to that already acquired. He is well on the way to becoming an independent reader, self-sufficient in using strategies when reading alone, helped by constant demonstration and reminders in the form of an adult's supportive actions.

6 REPHRASE IT

Rephrase the run-up to the problem word in more natural language.

TEXT: We were very poor and couldn't **afford** a barn.
SIMON: *'We were very poor and couldn't . . .'* [pause]
TEACHER: 'We were very poor and couldn't – something – a barn.'
SIMON: *'We were very poor and couldn't . . .'* [pause]
TEACHER: [rephrasing the run-up] 'We were so poor we couldn't – something – a barn.' [repeats] 'We were so poor we couldn't – something – a barn.'
SIMON: **Afford***!* [returns to the text and reads] *'We were very poor and couldn't afford a barn.'*

Simon could have been helped to build **afford**, but the adult was aware that he tended to rely exclusively on phonics, and the rephrasing route was chosen this time in the interest of maintaining a balance of cues. This formed part of a programme which aimed to extend his range of cues.

Book language is not the same as spoken language, and the difference between the two registers often acts as a barrier to the reading of a word, even when all the others in that sentence have been read correctly.

By rephrasing the run-up to the problem word, sometimes including the words beyond, and changing the bookish language to something more familiar, the adult can remove the barrier of the register.

In this example the text was changed from 'We were very poor and couldn't' to 'We were so poor we couldn't.'

Simon was helped by removing **and** (which separated two ideas), and replacing it with **so** (which connected the two ideas), thereby making it easier to appreciate the link of cause and effect. He was further helped by the connecting of the second **couldn't** with its subject **we**. The adult's rephrasing had changed the disjointed sentence into one unit of thought: 'We were so poor we couldn't – something – a barn.'

Listening to this more familiar register, Simon was able to draw on his own vocabulary and supply the word **afford**. Instantly recognizing that this matched the word on the page, he was now able to read it embedded in the original language of the book. It was at this point of returning **afford** to the actual text that Simon intuitively learned something about register. This is significant knowledge, to be carried into his own writing, where the purposes of different registers have to be explored in order to communicate effectively.

On this particular occasion the rephrasing was spoken, but it could be written down and placed beside the original in the text.

Our explanation makes explicit something which actually happens instinctively. We have dissected the exchange between Simon and his teacher because we want to show how and why it worked. The intuitive exchange lasted only a few seconds, but it contained elements known to be valuable for language learning:

- it was learning at the point of need;
- it worked at an implicit level.

Unfamiliar register, then, is a regular stumbling block for developing readers. It may well be responsible for loss of comprehension even where all the words have been read correctly, for example 'He bade him stay his hand'. Problems with register often come to the surface only when a word is proving difficult to read. Parents and helpers, who appreciate having the right 'tools' for the job, usually welcome being made aware of its impact, and being given some strategies to counteract it.

7 QUESTION IT

Turn a sentence round into a question (Hunt *et al.* 1985: 108).

Example 1

TEXT: Chip saw a bumble bee.
NAT: [turns page and pauses, concentrating on the picture of the bee which he had been talking about earlier]
TEACHER: [quietly, and in a tone indicating that she is engrossed in hearing the next line] What did Chip see?
NAT: [reading] *'Chip saw a bumble bee.'*

This is a way of solving a problem before it happens, while maintaining fluency. It is unobtrusive and confidence-building. It consists of taking the actual words of the sentence which the child is about to read, and reordering them as a question. The wording of the question should leave the reader no option but to frame his reply in the actual words of the text, including the potential problem word. For example, in the sentence 'Chip saw a bumble bee', the adult anticipated his habitual reversal problem with the word **saw**. By quietly whispering the question 'What did Chip see?' she helped tune him in to reading **saw** successfully, without interrupting his flow of reading.

Example 2

Because it is so important to keep the reading moving, the adult may even choose to go into the beginning of the expected answer by giving something of its opening.

TEXT: They swam underwater.
ADULT: Where did they swim? 'They sw . . .'

This supportive action often opens up a wider variety of problems, revealing other language needs – say, if **see'd** (Example 1) or **swimmed** (Example 2) were to be the child's responses.

Example 3

Sometimes the adult cannot know precisely just where the problem lies. In the following example, Phil was simply sitting and staring at this sentence:

TEXT: The wolf and the bear shook with fear.
ADULT: [fearfully] What did the wolf and the bear shake with?

This particular supportive action was used in preference to more detailed work on individual words, because it came near the beginning of the session. At that point the adult's overriding concern was to increase Phil's confidence by sustaining his fluency. Concerned to keep the reading going, and unsure exactly which word or words were the problem anyway, her question parcelled up and offered him all the words. She sensed that his hesitation was more a reluctance to take risks than a problem with the words, and her action removed the risk.

Example 4

Finally, an example in which the adult's question serves to narrow down the range of options possible after **nest**, by suggesting a description of place.

TEXT: He saw an old nest, high up in the green branches.
CHILD: 'He saw an old nest . . .' [pauses]
TEACHER: Where did he see an old nest?

It could well be that the child was reading on in his head, so the question may have served to confirm the meaning he was already picking up from the remainder of the sentence. If he had gone only as far as the word **up**, even that would have been significant in indicating a place.

8 RUN UP AND SAMPLE IT

Read up to, or up to and beyond, a problem word, phonically sampling the first bit of the word, using a natural pace and intonation.
   This strategy is useful whether the word is at the beginning, in the middle or at the end of a sentence.

Example 1

TEXT: Mum gave her a **special** birthday present. She took the paper off, and found a box inside. She opened the box and **suddenly** a jack-in-the-box popped out!

FRAN: *'Mum gave her a . . .'* [long pause]

TEACHER: 'Mum gave her a **spĕ** . . . birthday present.' [repeats] 'Mum gave her a **spe . . . e . . . e**' [holding the sound]

FRAN: **Special!** *'. . . special birthday present. She opened the box and* **s . . . s . . . s . . .**'

TEACHER: Keep going.

FRAN: [distracted by the problem, reading quite flatly] *'***s . . . s . . .** *some-thing. a. jack. in. the. box. popped. out.'*

TEACHER: [at a normal narrative pace and with expression, to convey sur-prise] 'She opened the box and **sud** . . . a jack-in-the-box popped out!' [repeats] 'She opened the box and **sud** . . . a jack-in-the-box popped out!'

FRAN: **Suddenly!** *'. . . suddenly a jack-in-the-box popped out.'*

When the adult demonstrates this technique for a child she is model-ling the most important strategy a child can use when reading indepen-dently. It is all-important because it pulls together such a wide range of cues.

It is something to be demonstrated and taught early on in Assisted reading, and consolidated throughout.

Because it is such an important strategy we provide two further illus-trations in which it is being consolidated.

The first example shows a child who, although coming towards the end of his Assisted reading stage and reading successfully most of the time, nevertheless finds himself puzzled by the word **obvious**.

Example 2

TEXT: When his parents asked what he was doing, Mallory replied 'Well, it's **obvious**, isn't it? I'm building a robot.'

NEAL: *'When his parents asked him what he was doing, Mallory replied "Well, it's . . ."'* [pause] *Mmmmm* . . . **ob, obv** . . . [pause] *'"Well, it's* **obv** *. . ."'* [pause]

TEACHER: [aware that **obv** is not a letter string usually found in English, but not commenting on that] Good thinking, Neal. I can see you're trying your run-up again, with a clever bit of building so far. Read a bit further, see if that helps.

NEAL: *'. . . "Well it's* **obv** *. . . isn't it"'* – **obvious!**

Neal halted at **obvious**, and chose to work on it. He spontaneously built it as far as **obv** but this phonic start was not sufficient to help him get the whole word. The supporting adult praised this tactic and prompted him to read on, to 'isn't it?'. Neal then went back and re-read the short sen-tence, this time reading **obvious**. – 'Well, it's obvious, isn't it?'

So what was the knowledge Neal needed in order to make use of all the other cues on offer, all the while keeping **obv** in mind?

• He needed to be knowledgeable about the different types of word which can follow **It's** . . . Perhaps, given the sentence, he was limiting himself to nouns: **robot . . ., machine . . .**

- When no noun appeared, he needed to be adaptable enough to go searching for more information further on in the text.
- He needed to know to always read on, because even the most insignificant words are part of the fabric of cues. Here 'isn't it?' clearly cued Neal in to the flavour of Mallory's way of talking. So . . .
- . . . he needed to have picked up on Mallory's precocious character from previous indications in the text.
- He needed the ability to complete the final check on **obvious** – in all probability a word he had never seen before – against the letters on the page.

Putting all these together, he had travelled from a phonic prompt, through contextual information, to a phonic clincher – the balanced range of cues which the adult had intended.

Furthermore, there had been an important moment of phonic learning. His recognition that **i.o.u.s.** represents the sounds of that unknown bit (. . . **ious**) of his problem word was an act of matching what he heard – a word previously confined to his oral vocabulary – to what he saw, the word on the page. As an incident of independent discovery, it is likely to make his acquisition of . . . **ious** memorable, perhaps all the more memorable because it will carry overtones of his enjoyment of Mallory's conceit.

The humour of the incident is likely to give impact to the phonic discovery, making it probable that he will read by analogy new words containing this phonic convention. And he is likely to reuse it in his own writing. (Yet another reason for using memorable literature.)

Example 3

This example illustrates once again the importance of balancing Broad and Fine tactics. Here the reading beyond the problem covers several sentences.

Matthew was reading about a boy searching library shelves for information about trees.

TEXT: There were **labels** on all the shelves. Some said 'COOKERY', others said 'SPORT', or 'GARDENING'.

MATTHEW: *'There were l.ă.b. lăb . . .'* [pause]

TEACHER: That's good, Matthew. You've taken the first sounds of that word and blended them together very well. Now read a bit further . . . in fact, keep going over that full stop there [pointing] into the next sentence. See if you can find more clues.

MATTHEW: *'There were – somethings – on all the shelves. Some said "COOKERY", others said "GARDENING".'* *It's those things that they put on shelves to tell you what books are.*

TEACHER: Good. You've spotted the **s** ending. You know there's more than one of these things. OK. Now have a look at that word again [pointing to **labels**; pause] Well now. See if you can remember something about the sounds of vowels. Remember when we wrote them all out like this? [she writes **a e i o u** on her pad to show him, and they have a short discussion about the fact that each can represent more than one sound] Now try this bit again [points to word]

MATTHEW: **lăb** . . .

TEACHER: What about the other sound for that **a**? Try 'There were **lā** . . . on all the shelves . . .'

MATTHEW: **lā** . . . **lāb** . . . **labels***!*

Matthew did not have the advantage enjoyed by Neal with his sample of **obv** because, crucially, he lacked the phonic knowledge demanded by the first syllable of his problem word **label**.

However, his teacher provided this Fine knowledge through phonic teaching in context, together with reminders to ensure that other Broad knowledge was brought in as reinforcement.

Matthew's first hold-up came at **labels**, which, using the run-up-and-sample-it strategy, he sounded out initially as **l.ă.b** . . . **lăb**. His teacher praised his blending ability but, realizing what cues lay ahead, discussed with him how sentences as well as words link together to make meaning. She prompted him to continue reading beyond the full stop, and on through the following sentence. Matthew had now read: 'There were **somethings** on all the shelves. Some said "COOKERY", others said "SPORT", or "GARDENING".' This gave him four clues:

• he realized shelves were involved;
• he remembered why words are sometimes written in capitals;
• he knew the problem word was plural;
• he knew the problem word referred to articles 'on all the shelves'.

The combined knowledge of these four pieces of information led him to say: 'It's those things they put on shelves that tell you what books are.'

A return to the problem word, however, proved unsuccessful. Matthew was not yet sufficiently flexible to give a trial to each sound of **a** as he considered this new word. He was hooked on **ă**, and so could not move away from **lăb** . . .. His teacher realized that some revision of putting phonic knowledge to practical use was needed, and reminded him of previous work on the two sounds of **a**, short and long. Then from his teacher's demonstration, he tried **lā** . . . and immediately he got it: '**lā** . . . **lāb** . . . **label***!*'

Phonic learning is at its most meaningful at these points of real use, a principle regularly applied in Assisted reading sessions.

In addition, acquiring phonic knowledge calls for extensive work which must take place outside these one-to-one Assisted reading sessions, where, in this case, Matthew would learn:

• the long and short sounds of the single vowels (extending this later to include other sounds, for example **a** as in **father**);
• competence in identifying the first single vowel in any word (vowel digraphs will be dealt with on other occasions);
• confidence to try out both possibilities for the first single vowel in any problem word of this type.

Matthew was beginning to realize that reading includes not only roving across sentences transferring meaning to and fro, but also juggling sounds to try out a range of phonic possibilities until meaning and phonics match.

9 HELP TO BUILD IT

Example 1

Help the child to look for the way to build any word for which there are no meaning cues at all.

TEXT: [caption to picture] This beetle is a cardinal beetle.
JAMES: *I don't know what that says.* [pointing to **cardinal**]
TEACHER: Well, what does that say? [pointing to **beetle**]
JAMES: **Beetle**
TEACHER: Well now, if that [pointing to **cardinal**] is coming in front of **beetle**, it's probably telling us something about it.
JAMES: *It's its name, I think.*
TEACHER: So do I. What kinds of beetle do you know?
JAMES: *Ladybird . . . cockroach . . . don't know any more . . . Oh, stag beetle?*
TEACHER: So . . . does that say **stag**? No. Well, I think because we have no other clues at all, we'll have to have a go at building this. See anything in it there that you know?
JAMES: **Car . . . card . . .**
TEACHER: Go on.
JAMES: **card . . . in . . . al . . . cardinál?**
TEACHER: [giving pronunciation] **Cárdinal**. That's right. Well done. 'This beetle is a cardinal beetle.'

James has learned a fact about beetles via a wholly phonic attack. **Cardinal** belongs to that small category of words to which the reader is unable to bring either prior knowledge or information from context.

Within that category there are technical terms (for example cardinal, sprocket, yomping), nonsense words (for example jellypoop, grunnion), and proper nouns (for example Sebastian, Rumania).

Example 2

Where context is lost because several difficult words cluster together, the supporting adult will have to select the word she considers to be the most buildable for a particular reader, using this as a trigger to unlock the rest.

TEXT: In the heat of the jungle he dreamed of the **thirst-quenching flavour** of **vanilla ice-cream**.
JODIE: *'In the heat of the jungle he dreamed of the . . .'* [pause]

TEACHER: Can you read on?

JODIE: [looking ahead, shakes head]

TEACHER: Show me those words you can read, up to the full stop.

JODIE: [laughing] **of**!

TEACHER: Well, that's a start. [selects a word she knows he has written in recent work] Look at this one [points to **ice**] You wrote this when you were writing about the Arctic on Monday.

JODIE: *Ah . . .* **ice**. *Oh!* **ice-cream**!

TEACHER: [selecting **vanilla** as buildable for Jodie] I think you can build this one. Try it.

JODIE: **Van . . . ill . . . vanill . . . vanilla**. *Vanilla ice-cream.*

TEACHER: OK, now you've read all this: 'In the heat of the jungle he dreamed of the . . . something something something . . . of vanilla ice-cream.' Let's tackle this one [selecting **thirst** as phonically possible for Jodie] Can you see any parts you know?

JODIE: *I know that* [pointing to **th**] *and I know that . . .* **st**.

TEACHER: And don't forget **i** and **r** work together to say **ir**, like **u.r.** and **e.r.** OK, then. **ir**?

JODIE: **thir . . . st . . . thirst**.

TEACHER: And **thirst** is joined onto this one with a hyphen like **ice** and **cream** – so these two words go together. Have a go . . . 'thirst-quen . . .' [she is supporting him more now in order to sustain this intensive work, orchestrating all the cues]

JODIE: *Opal fruits in that advert! . . . er . . . wait a minute . . . thirst-quench-ing!*

TEACHER: 'He dreamed of the thirst-quenching – something – of vanilla ice-cream' [pauses; no response from Jodie]

TEACHER: [providing even more scaffolding] . . . 'the thirst-quenching fl . . . of vanilla ice-cream'

JODIE: **flăv . . .?**

TEACHER: [pen under the **a**] Does that letter *always* say **ă**?

JODIE: **flā . . . flāv . . . flavour**!

TEACHER AND JODIE TOGETHER: [triumphantly] 'In the heat of the jungle he dreamed of the thirst-quenching flavour of vanilla ice-cream.'

10 WAIT AND SEE

When a child continues reading past a misread word, wait, to give him opportunity to self-correct from information further on in the text.

Example 1

TEXT: It was his **wicked** uncle who was king at that time. This bad man had sent Ali to prison, where . . .

JACK: *'It was his wickt –*

TEACHER: [does not interrupt]

JACK: – *uncle who was king at that time. This bad man had sent Ali to prison, where . . .'* Ah! [self-corrects] *'. . . wicked uncle'!* [re-reads] *'It was his wicked uncle who was king at that time . . .'*

TEACHER: [quickly and unobtrusively, hardly interrupting] Well done. You did that yourself. Good.

JACK: [continues] *'. . . This bad man had sent Ali to prison, where . . .'* [teacher makes note to comment on **icked** later]

Waiting for a self-correction is actually much more difficult than offering immediate assistance, such as launching into word-building or supplying the correct pronunciation. When a child has built part of the word successfully and is so nearly right, there is an instinctive urge to keep things tidy. However, there are powerful reasons why 'wait and see' is not the absence of support which it might at first appear.

A significant feature in this episode is the fact that Jack, unlike readers in our previous examples, did not halt at the problem word but carried on reading fluently, not only to the end of the sentence but on into the next. This influenced the teacher's decision to 'wait and see', along with her recognition that

- the **wick** in **wickt** represented 50 per cent phonic success;
- Jack's pronunciation of the ending as **t** reflected knowledge of the usual **icked** pronunciation;
- **bad man** and **prison** would provide useful information.

She was right in thinking that his speed of reading would enable him to reach the cues ahead while he still had recall of **wickt**.

Jack's original **wickt** was perfectly understandable. He had intuitively seen the word as a verb (because of the **ed** ending) and said it as **wickt** by analogy with **tricked**, **picked**, etc. The teacher praised that thinking and explained that **wicked** is an exception. She left him with two impressions:

- he had done well: his phonic knowledge on this point was really very good, alongside which he had been flexible enough to modify it when content indicated;
- a good reader stays alert to the tricks the English language can play.

Example 2

TEXT: A long rope tied the donkey to the fence. It was **strange** and puzzling that no one had been back yet to set him free. Today was Monday, and . . .

BOBBIE: *'A long rope tied the donkey to the fence. It was strangling* [teacher decides to 'wait and see'] *and puzzling that no one had been back yet to set him free. Today was Monday, and . . .'*

TEACHER: Whoa! Hang on a minute. 'It was strangling and puzzling . . .' That doesn't sound right, does it? Let's go back to this bit. Read that bit again [pointing to 'It was strange']

BOBBIE: *'It was* **strang** . . .'
TEACHER: I can see what you're getting at. You're thinking about that rope, aren't you? *And* you've got the initial blend right . . . **str** . . .

By this point in the interaction, the teacher and Bobbie had arrived at a situation from which she could take any one of a number of supportive actions.

Waiting is even more difficult when the child shows no signs of self-correcting after continuing quite some way, but 'wait and see' remains a helpful action even when a child does not self-correct. A child should still have opportunity to carry on reading beyond a misread word because:

• further information may trigger a self-correction;
• it places the responsibility for correction with the child;
• it presents the adult with insights into his cueing development;
• if he does manage to self-correct, disruption is avoided.

The timing of when to intervene is not governed by hard and fast rules. In this episode the teacher decided to stop the reading part way into the next sentence, which is probably the earliest point at which to step in. Earlier than that, the reader has not had a chance to pick up enough relevant information. On the other hand, the intervention point may be quite a few sentences ahead, or even at the end of the page. It depends on how significant for comprehension the misread word is, and whether there is a possibility that self-correction might still take place.

So, to summarize, the 'wait' in 'wait and see' is a positive supportive action. It is positive because every successful self-correction:

• proves to the child that he can carry phonics and meaning across a span of text until they both accurately match the word on the page;
• is a powerful experience of both phonic consolidation (for example Jack's **wick** in **wicked**) and phonic acquisition (for example the **ed** in **wicked**);
• builds confidence;
• is a step on the road to independence.

Part 5 Phonic knowledge within reading

Throughout all those episodes two aspects constantly featured:

• readers were expected to integrate their phonic knowledge with other cues;
• there were references to phonic work taking place outside the sessions.

In effect, this was implicitly addressing two crucial questions, which we shall now consider in greater depth:

- How should phonic instruction be integrated into real reading situations?
- What other phonic teaching is needed to support this?

How should phonic instruction be integrated into real reading situations?

The episodes we have presented should go a long way in providing the answer to this first question. In them we see phonic instruction used at the point of real need in practical, problem-solving word attack. This helps the reader to perform that necessary juggling act of holding meaning in his mind while at the same time using phonic information to generate a word to match with the printed word in front of him.

There is an emphasis in the supportive actions on extracting as much information as possible from context. This may appear to subordinate phonics. Actually the opposite is true: that emphasis operates to ensure that children use phonic cues to best effect, precisely because they are tightly and indispensably interwoven as part of the overall network of cues. The phonic cues may not appear as toweringly obvious as in exclusively phonic approaches to word attack, but in fact their very integration makes their learning all the more secure.

Integrating phonic instruction into reading situations provides two benefits for the learner:

- motivation – through regular experience of using existing phonic knowledge for real purposes;
- discovery of new phonic knowledge – born directly out of the problem-solving which utilized known phonic knowledge.

What other phonic teaching is needed?

A child's acquisition of phonic knowledge rests on his wider phonological awareness (see Chapters 1 and 2). This awareness is greatly helped by early oral experience of rhyme, alliteration, poems and stories, and it holds the key to later success when the learner comes to analyse the print representation of words (phonics). The development of this earlier purely oral/aural knowledge depends on the child possessing good listening skills and the adult giving sufficient time to teaching and demonstration. Adults need to know that time spent 'playing' with sounds can make all the difference between the skill of reading being acquired smoothly or not. There is as great a need for systematic and informed work in that area as now, when the printed representations of sounds are studied. And, importantly at that early stage, children need to feel that manipulating and playing with sounds is fun, enjoyable and interesting. Once established, that attitude and that flexibility will be brought into the later stages of word study.

Of all the technical terms connected with reading, phonics is the most emotive, even among those members of the public not actually involved in teaching. It is the term most closely connected with calls of 'back to basics', and the one most likely to prompt the taking up of entrenched positions. However, the term usually seems to encompass only phonic facts – just one aspect of an area of learning which actually has three parts:

* phonic facts
* phonic skills
* applied phonics.

PHONIC FACTS

By 'phonic facts' we mean the elements of the English coding system, and they are constant for both reading and writing. 'Code' suggests a simple correspondence between its written symbols and the sounds they represent. The English coding system, however, is not quite so straightforward. There are some 44 sounds (phonemes) in the spoken English language, and the alphabet's 26 letters are not sufficient to represent all of them on a one-to-one basis. Some sounds therefore have to be denoted by combinations of letters (for example **sh**). However, the complications do not stop there, because some phonemes may be represented in a variety of ways (for example **ay**, **ai**, **a-e** as in **gate**), and some written symbols-of-sounds (graphemes) represent a number of phonemes (for example **y** in **my**, **happy** and **year**). It is estimated that there are some 220 graphemes to be learned overall, and these can be found classified in various charts of phoneme–grapheme correspondence, including Gattegno (1962) and, more recently, THRASS (Davies and Ritchie 1998).

Arriving at an order

The teaching of phonic facts, by which we mean these phoneme–grapheme correspondences, should be pinned to a structured school-wide scheme of work which orders the progressive introduction of the 200-plus graphemes. There are strong arguments that the sequence of their introduction is a matter for each school, and it is important that all members of staff be involved in the construction of this order. It is their discussion towards a final choice which will give them an understanding of its underlying structure. Decisions – such as whether common vowel digraphs are to be introduced alongside consonant digraphs (**oo**, **ee**, **ar** and **ai**, perhaps with **ch**, **sh**, **th**), in which year to introduce 'magic e', or even whether to call it 'magic e' or 'modifying e' – need to be discussed in an open and relaxed manner. It is worth allowing time for one or two staff sessions in which people feel free to admit to any gaps in their knowledge, and can come to recognize that there *is* no definitive order. Although they may have recourse to various recommendations, for example from the DfEE or from the order built into whatever published reading scheme the school might be using, when teachers as a staff have the confidence to explore freely for themselves their preferred order, the consequent ownership will greatly enhance their teaching. Once an order of grapheme introduction has been arrived at through such consultation, there is an increased likelihood that every teacher will carry the framework in her head.

Teaching the phonic facts via two complementary approaches

This framework then gives her the essential basis for teaching the phonic facts via two different but complementary approaches. These parallel streams of learning are:

- a proactive systematic programme which introduces and teaches phoneme–grapheme correspondence;
- the opportunistic teaching of phonic facts within all the ongoing reading and writing situations.

Neither one is satisfactory by itself. A purely formal proactive phonic programme is unlikely to motivate a child, if all it does is squeeze him down one narrow learning path. If it does not start off from a point of need, or is not based on a question a child has asked, there is a danger that he will not see any practical application for the phonic facts. On the other hand, a purely opportunistic approach may leave some children progressing through their schooling with patchy knowledge. What we are recommending is a spine of proactive work delivered whole-class and consolidated in group and individual work, which interacts continually with reactive work arising from the reading and writing of the moment.

In other words, each class each term will work at an agreed prescribed section of the spine. But at the same time, for instance, that teacher who may be dealing with consonant blends as her term's work (**cr**, **dr**, **cl**, **fl**, etc.) should in no way be precluded from:

- helping Christopher with the hard **ch** sound at the beginning of his name and with **ph**;
- guiding Linda to see that **stegosaurus** has four syllables;
- showing Anne that the **e** at the end of her name does no work at all, likening it to the **e** at the end of **house**, **have** and **come**.

Teachers confident from having helped to construct their proactive order are able to *depart* from the framework whenever class or individual needs demand.

Whole-class work

We will now consider ideas for whole-class teaching of the school's agreed proactive spine for the progressive introduction of graphemes.

Whatever the age- and ability group, the principles remain the same:

- through direct teaching the children are presented with a group of phonic facts;
- these are to be learned in a fixed period of time – say, a term or a half-term;
- there is a range of whole-class activities designed to teach these phonic facts;
- there is a bank of phonic resources for individual and group consolidation work.

Whole-class activities

The whole-class activities designed to teach phonic facts can be effectively centred around displays appropriate to the learning stage of the class, for instance:

- an alphabet frieze;
- a collection table featuring objects beginning with the same consonant blend;
- a cluster of mobiles, each illustrating a different vowel digraph in a related group: **ar**, **ir**, **or** (this is how Jodie in supportive action 9 was introduced to **ir**);
- a word bank of common suffixes: . . . **tion**, . . . **ment**, . . . **ure**.

Other activities might include:

- class/group display of illustrated sentences or captions, depending on the place of the class on the 'spine', for example
  – illustrating alliteration: 'a brilliant bright brown brick bridge'
  – illustrating rime: 'I wish for a fish in a dish', 'he stole a mole from its hole'
  – illustrating homophone pairs: hair/hare, dear/deer;
- the five-minute whole-class quiz ('Who'll be first out to play today?', 'Who can show me, somewhere on the wall, a vowel digraph with a **u** in it?', 'Who can tell me a word which begins with a three-consonant blend?');
- oral games, for example 'I went to market and I bought a shell . . . ship . . . shaving cream . . . sugar . . . shells . . .'chute', or a round-the-class story featuring words sharing a common sound: 'You start, Alan': [Alan] *'Silly Sally'* . . . [Jimmy] *'saw some'* [Ann] *'sausages sizzling'* . . . etc.;
- the production, over the course of a week, of a wall list built up of words added by the children from their own reading or writing: 'If you find a word with **ough** in it write it on our list.' This can form the basis of the weekly spelling homework, the teacher choosing five words from the list, and each child adding five more of his own choice;
- five-minute brainstorming to develop self-reliance and flexibility: 'How many ways can you think of to write ā?', 'How many sounds can **ough** make?'

A bank of phonic resources for consolidation work

It is important to have a good resource bank, selected from the wealth of commercially available resources and supplemented by school-made additions: games, paper and pencil activities including wordsearches and crossword puzzles, IT activities, plastic letter activities, learning letter strings through handwriting activities.

However, such resources should not be used as replacements for the necessary supported direct teaching. When this happens it can leave the learner feeling solitary and baffled as to the purpose and application of what he is doing.

Even where phonic resources are being used for consolidation in carefully linked ways, teachers must still be wary of the assumption that successfully completed phonic activities will necessarily mean successful application of phonic facts in situations of real use.

Individual follow-up work

Tony's teacher in supportive action 2 reminded him at the end of his Assisted reading session of other **ci** . . . words: **cinema**, **city**, **cigar**, **cinder** – all of which had featured in a class display the previous term. She also arranged for a complementary wordsearch activity, which was revision of **ce** . . . during the classroom language hour.

Neal's teacher (supportive action 8) told the whole class about his discovery of **ious**, suggesting this become their 'pattern of the week' and that they make a 'detective list' of any more words they could find with that pattern.

These two examples demonstrate the value of follow-up work from Assisted reading sessions and reading at home. Other individual input may occur when a teacher is aware that a child's forthcoming reading requires knowledge of a certain sound, perhaps when she knows a particular book in a reading scheme is coming up.

Each child should keep a store or personal record of the phonic facts he is working on. Its format may vary. For instance, it can be in the form of a phonic wall showing the phonic facts targeted for the term, one grapheme per brick to be coloured in when he can show he has used it in reading or writing. Or it can be a notebook or file, with each page headed by an illustrated trigger word for a phonic fact, and other similar words collected below (see Tony's 'cinema' page in supportive action 2, page 95). As many of these words will have been collected from his writing, so it becomes a reference list, as well as learning-consolidation.

To summarize, then, the teaching of phonic facts has to be delivered in four ways:

Proactive Whole class	Reactive Whole class
Proactive Individual and group	Reactive Individual and group

PHONIC SKILLS

It is imperative that these phonic skills are accorded the same importance as phonic facts. This is because, although phonic facts can be taught in isolation, they cannot fulfil the purpose for which they are being taught unless, through the vehicle of phonic skills, they are connected to language in use. Any reference to the teaching of phonics which does not include this skills component is seriously incomplete.

So, the appropriately phased introduction of these skills should be part of each school's proactive spine of phonic teaching, with each teacher also being ready and able to develop them reactively.

By 'phonic skills' we mean the following cluster of understandings, attitudes and abilities:

1 an understanding that there are good practical reasons for learning phonics;
2 an understanding that this language of ours *appears* to play tricks, and that the coding has its weaknesses;
3 a flexible attitude, being brave enough to consider the range of phonic options for a word;
4 an ability to test phonics speedily against context, and vice versa;
5 an ability to recognize and articulate what finally clinched a word choice (metacognition);
6 an understanding of the role of consonants in word attack;
7 an understanding of the role of vowels in word attack;
8 an understanding of the role of syllables in word attack;
9 an ability to make use of letter-string analogies between words;
10 an ability to sequence sounds smoothly (blending and building);
11 an ability to recognize phonic elements at speed, developing automaticity;
12 an ability to talk about phonics using the correct terminology.

Their development is promoted by a combination of:

• direct teaching (for example, for the role of vowels);
• demonstration (for example, for testing phonics against context);
• an ongoing classroom climate of expectations and reminders (for example, for understanding that phonics have practical applications).

We offer below practical suggestions for the development of each of these 12 phonic skills.

1 An understanding that there are good practical reasons for learning phonics

This first understanding can only develop from a classroom climate in which connections are constantly being made between the separate learning of phonics and their uses in helping to solve real problems. So, although some specific teaching time will be allocated to it, equally important are the incidental references daily interwoven into all classroom activity. The making of these connections depends largely on the teacher's being able to utilize opportunities as they arise. By seizing on incidental chances for demonstration, and by focusing on children's positive uses of phonic cues (both in Assisted reading sessions and in class), she continually highlights the place of phonics.

- 'Well done, Matthew . . . **labels** . . . yes. You remembered all that work we did before the holiday about the sounds of vowels. You remembered that if ă didn't fit you could try ā . . . vowels have more than one sound, don't they?'
- 'Michael's chosen this book from the library shelf [*George Speaks* by Dick King-Smith]. But he hasn't worked out yet what it's called . . . can we help him read its title? Who can remember what **g** says when there's an **e** next? Remember? [writing on board] **page** . . . **cage** . . . **stage**?'
- 'Blue group are going to make a model of a castle. Ah! **castle** . . . now that's a word in this term's word bank, isn't it . . . from the . . . **s.t.l.e** list, remember?'
- On a 'phonic walk' around the school looking at notices and work on display, Leo and his helper found . . . **tion** in **Reception**, **construction**, **competition** and **addition**.

2 An understanding that this language of ours *appears* to play tricks, and that the coding has its weaknesses

Likewise, this second understanding also requires a background of a shared classroom assumption, this time the assumption that our language *appears* to play tricks. A kind of good-humoured tolerance needs to be cultivated in the children for the fact that our coding is not straightforward: **maid, raid, braid, said, plaid.** Jack, in supportive action 10, was able to take **wicked** in his stride because he had already learned to appreciate the code's apparently quirky behaviour.

In addition, the teacher should plan regular but brief sessions for learning about interesting categories of words:

- foreign derivations (yacht, khaki, blitz);
- words derived from names of people (bunsen, dahlia, wattage);
- interesting derivations (salary, tawdry, quiz);
- words with visually similar patterns but sounding different (home-women-come; stomach-machine; eat-weather-theatre).

Children can be encouraged to devise various presentations for groups of words which interest them. One might be a wall-collection in two columns:

'mildly crazy words'	*'really crazy words'*
any	ocean
guitar	busy
	pterodactyl
	psalm

From her pupils' healthy discussion as to which words are 'crazy' and to what degree, the teacher will be able to learn much about their phonic knowledge. Following up the whole-class discussion in which the pupils justify particular placements, she can explain that none of the words are, in fact, 'crazy' at all, but that the apparent irregularities arise from a variety of word origins. She can select some of the words for more detailed exploration of their backgrounds, with Ayto's (1990) *Dictionary of Word Origins* (Bloomsbury Press), and Beal's (1991) *Book of Words* (Kingfisher) being useful additions to a staffroom's collection of teacher resources.

3 A flexible attitude, being brave enough to consider the range of phonic options for a word

There is a natural link here with writing, where children are encouraged to have a go and experiment with their spellings, and in which the teacher holds back from giving a spelling until the child has done so.

It is productive to encourage children to try out combinations for themselves. Trial-and-error experimentation, or 'what if' thinking, can be individually or whole-class led. It not only helps the acquisition of phonic facts, because discovery is powerful, but it also promotes the exploratory frame of mind so essential to self-reliant use of phonic cues.

A number of entertaining games and activities are possible to encourage 'what if' thinking. For instance:

- the five-minute brainstorm again (see page 111): 'How many consonants can form a blend with **r**?', 'What happens if we team **o** with **y**?'
- Using a sentence well within the children's reading capability, for example 'A sn**ow** b**all** hit me on the h**ead**', ask the children to read it in alternative pronunciations: **ow** as in **cow**, **all** as **ă**, **head** as **heed**.
- Ask the children to collect trade names which use phonically alternative spelling, for example Kleeneze, Bettaware, Supasava.
- Ask them to invent their own trade names for a shop display.
- Ask them to find new ways to spell their own names (Shakespeare did).
- Ask them to find as many words as possible to complete a given consonant-plus-vowel opening, for example **ba**: **bad, bar, bay, ball, bare, baulk, ballerina**.

However useful these separated activities may be, their relevance to problem-solving in reading needs constant reinforcement. In brief whole-class teaching sessions, the teacher can model the word-solving of certain words in sentences on the board or OHP, demonstrating how flexibility can be used in practice. By 'modelling' we mean the teacher talking her thoughts out loud as though she were a learner meeting the difficult word for the first time. For instance, taking the sentence: 'The old woman went to get the **dough** for the day's bread', her monologue might go something like this:

'Here's a strange word ... **o.u.g.h** ... is that like **enough**? "the duff for the day's bread". No, that doesn't sound like a word I've heard before.

Cough, then? . . . "the doff for the day's bread" . . . I need to keep trying other possibilities . . . What else do I know? **Thought** . . . "the dor for the day's bread". **Through**? "the doo for the day's bread"? That sounds nearly familiar . . . hang on . . . **Though** – yes . . . "the dough for the day's bread" . . . Yes! I remember my mum baking bread with dough . . . bit like Play-Doh really.'

After this, she can get the children working similarly on another sentence.

4 An ability to test phonics speedily against context, and vice versa

The reader who can hold contextual information in mind at the same time as he considers a word's phonics, and who can hold onto phonic information while searching for contextual appropriateness, is nearing the end of the Assisted reading stage and approaching independence.

A great deal of work during the Assisted reading sessions helps to develop this facility (see Fran, Neal and Matthew in supportive action 8). However, it is also important to demonstrate it in whole-class sessions.

A major component of this whole-class work is the training of pupils to provide a word missing from a sentence – GAP time (Give A Possibility time). The teacher has to make choices about three aspects of the task (and there is progression possible within each), namely:

easy	*difficult*
oral	print-based
place gap at end of sentence	place gap at beginning of sentence
omit the whole word	provide some letters. The addition of phonic information makes the task more specific, requiring greater accuracy and reducing opportunities for inventiveness

So, brief but frequent oral sessions comprise work such as Figure 4.20. These examples were all oral, but of course just as frequently similar examples should be written (on OHP, flipchart or board) and worked upon in exactly the same way. Children, too, can compose examples for each other.

Figure 4.20   GAP (Give A Possibility) time

Teacher	Class response
Six sentences in GAP time today . . . Finish my sentence for me . . . no letter clues at first, so lots of possibilities:	
'I was really afraid of the savage **something**'	beast, creature, dog, monster, teacher
OK. Now here's one a little bit harder, because the missing word is in the middle; you've got to hold on to two bits of information, one each side of the gap: 'The day was cold and **something**, so I put on my wellington boots'	rainy, snowy, stormy, wet, bad
Now the hardest kind of gap . . . at the beginning. No clues to help you before you get to the word. '**Something** litter was left after the fair had gone'	shocking, nasty, disgusting, considerable, only *'lots of' was praised for its meaning, but reluctantly disallowed as being more than one word*
Now here are three more sentences. This time I'm going to give you some letter clues, but just because you've got letters, don't stop thinking about the rest of the sentence. 'Janet's birthday is in **JJJJJJJJ** . . .' I'll give you the next sound . . . **Juuuuu** . . . All right, now here comes the third sound: **Julllll** . . .	January, June, July June, July July!
Here's one with the missing word in the middle: 'She heard a **sssss** . . . sound at the door' 'She heard a **sccccccc** . . . sound at the door' 'She heard a **scrrrrr** . . . sound at the door' 'She heard a **scraaaa** . . . sound at the door'	strange, scratching, scary, soft, screaming scraping, suspicious, singing, sudden, silly, slippery, sizzling scary, scratching, scuffling, screaming scratching, screaming scratching!

Teacher	Class response
Now the hardest . . . a beginning word . . . **'Nnnn** . . . lions came round the tent at night'	now, naughty, nice, nine, no, nervous
'Nor . . . lions came round the tent at night' **'Norm** . . . lions came round the tent at night'	naughty normally!

Constant reminders are needed that GAP time is not just an interlude of isolated games, but is helping to develop a skill children must use in their own reading; a skill so important that they should receive praise when they do so.

So naturally they are going to need support to continue using the self-same strategies they have been using for gaps – concentrating on context, using a minimal amount of phonics – when there is in fact no gap at all, but a challenging word in print. Therefore there should be whole-class teaching sessions, like the GAP times, where these skills are applied to text.

One element common to all these activities is the usefulness of being able to work at speed. This can be communicated to a large extent by the teacher's example in reading and re-reading the sentence fluently, quickly moving to and fro between contextual and phonic references. Valuable textual experience can be provided by material drawn from other areas of the curriculum.

(Crosswords and wordsearches offer complementary practice of the same skill of balancing meaning and letters to find an appropriate fit. In addition, the well-known games of Junior Scrabble and Hangman – played electronically on a Franklin Spellmaster or traditionally on board or paper – entertain while exercising awareness of phonic possibilities and prediction of letter strings.)

5 An ability to recognize and articulate what finally clinched a word choice (metacognition)

Metacognition – the understanding and articulation of the thinking processes involved in problem-solving – is an ability which reinforces and consolidates learning. The manner in which Tammy is able to discuss what had clinched her word choice is a skill worth promoting.

TEXT: Her mother came and caught her/And smacked her naughty daughter

TAMMY: *'Her mother came and caught her/And smacked her* [pause] *nnnn . . . er . . . daughter. And smacked her nnnnn . . .'* [pause] **naughty**! *naughty daughter*

TEACHER: Well done. How did you know that was **naughty**?

TAMMY: *Well, first I wasn't sure about that* [pointing to **daughter**], *but then I knew it 'cos it rhymed, and it's her* <u>mother</u> *who smacks her, and then I saw these letters – look –* [pointing to **augh** in **naughty**]*, and so I knew it was like* **daughter***, so I just built it . . . I know that* **y** *says* **i** *at the end of a word. And anyway, if you're good you don't get smacked.*

The development of this phonic skill may be supported in the following ways:

- by the teacher modelling for the class or group 'how to be a reading detective' (like Tammy);
- by having groups or the whole class working together on a paragraph from which two or three words have been wholly deleted, or partially deleted leaving some phonic cues – crucial to this activity is the discussion which follows it, justifying the reasons for their choices;
- by prompting and supporting explanations of 'working out' within Assisted reading sessions;
- by the means of supportive questioning the adult enables the child to verbalize his working out of certain problem words. His articulation of his successful cueing routes acts as consolidation, and her response to that gives a seal of approval to his strategies:
  - 'That was good thinking. Which word(s) on that page gave you the clue about this word on this page?'
  - 'Excellent! The angry giant. How did you know **angry**? [child points to picture] So why didn't you say **cross** or **mad**?' *"Cos there's not a* **c** *or* **m.***'*
  - 'You're getting very good at keeping going. How many words did you have to read, before you found your clue?'
  - 'That's great! You got that without going through all the letters in the word, I think. So tell me, which letters did you use?'

6 An understanding of the role of consonants in word attack

Consonant learning comprises facts and strategies, and both should be integrated into the school's proactive spine of phonic knowledge.

Facts about consonants

This learning can be divided into four:

- single consonants,
- consonant blends,
- consonant digraphs (**ch, sh, th, ph, wh**),
- silent consonants (**kn, wr, gn,** . . . **mb**).

Consonants and their blends are overwhelmingly constant in their representation of phonemes (the only three exceptions being **s** as in **sure**, and soft **c** and **g**).

It is important to teach consonant blends as whole units, for example **cr** not **c** + **r**, **bl** not **b** + **l**.

The learning of initial consonant blends is made less daunting once it is realized that 25 of the existing 29 can be straightforwardly presented in just three groups, two based on the second letters **l** and **r**, and a group beginning with **s**:

blends with **l**: **bl, cl, fl, gl, pl, sl**
blends with **r**: **br, cr, dr, fr, gr, pr, tr**
blends beginning with **s**: **sc, sk, sl, sm, sn, sp, st, sw, scr, spl, spr, str**

In practice, once a child has learned some eight to ten blends, the concept has usually been understood and, generalizing from that, he learns the rest quite quickly.

Strategies for using consonants in word attack

Consonants can convey a word, even without the word's vowels. The security which children gain from the realization of the trustworthiness of consonants can support their further training in the following strategies:

- looking for all the consonants before the first vowel, safe in the knowledge that they will yield reliable information – unlike the complexity of vowel combinations;

    The more consonants there are in the minimal sample the more the options for the word are reduced. This was illustrated by the teacher on page 117, who gradually narrowed down the possibilities for the missing word **scratching**:

s   produced 12 responses from the class;
sc   produced 4 responses;
scr   produced 2 responses;
scra   produced the 1 response which was the word.

    Such work is usefully rounded off by the teacher pointing out the proportion of letters needed to get the whole word: 'You only needed four out of nine! Great!'
- taking the consonant or consonant-blend back to the sentence to link it with contextual information.
- using all available consonant knowledge, especially when the vowels are being difficult.

    It is possible to read the following sentence: 'The ch—rch st—d on the h—ll, and they h—rd the b—lls r—ng out.' This is an indication of the strength of consonants to convey words even without their vowels. Children benefit by practising this skill. Sentences may be quickly written in this manner on the board or OHP, or children can invent them for each other.

    (Interestingly, this is very similar to written work produced by children at a certain developmental stage in spelling, before their understanding of vowels has emerged – further illustration of the power of consonants.)

7 An understanding of the role of vowels in word attack

Vowels are often the particularly puzzling element in a problem word, and children should be helped to appreciate just how crucial they are. The understanding they need is twofold, comprising facts about vowels, and strategies for making good use of them in word attack.

This understanding can be taught directly, appropriately integrated into phonic facts teaching along the proactive spine.

Facts about vowels

- There are five basic vowels: **a**, **e**, **i**, **o**, **u**.
- **y** is a special case, to be considered as the sixth vowel, because:
  - it also works as a consonant
    (There is justification for presenting **y** as a vowel from the start, in the fact that there are only some 40 or so words in frequent use which begin with **y** working as a consonant: yacht, yak, yam, yank, yap, yard, yarn, yawn, year, yearn, yeast, yell, yellow, yelp, yen, yes, yesterday, yet, yew, yield, yodel, yoga, yoke, yolk, yon, yonder, you, you'll, you're, you've, young, youngster, your, yours, yourself, youth, yowl, yo-yo, yucca, yuck, yule.)
  - it always duplicates the sound of another vowel, **i**.
- A vowel sound is made through a completely open mouth (and larynx) . . . neither throat, tongue, teeth nor lips block the flow of air.
- There is one vowel sound (basic vowel or vowel digraph) in every syllable,
- so there is at least one vowel sound (as above) in every word.
- There are some 23 vowel phonemes in our language, and only six basic vowels: this means that some of the 23 phonemes have to be represented by graphemes which are combinations of letters.
- These combinations of letters form six main groups:
  - the vowels double up: **oo**, **ee**
  - they pair up: **ai**, **au**, **ea**, **ei**, **oa**, **oi**, **ou**, **ue**
  - they pair up with **r**, **w** and **y**: **ar**, **er**, **ir**, **or**, **ur**; **aw**, **ew**, **ow**; **ay**, **ey**, **oy**, **uy**
  - some of these doubles and pairs team up into threes with **r**: **oor**, **eer**, **air**, **ear**, **oar**, **our**
  - there are some teams with **gh**: **igh**, **ough**, **augh**
  - vowels modified by **e** ('magic e').
- To make matters more complicated, they often 'swap jobs'; for instance, the **o** in **women** saying **i**, the **a** in **any** saying **e**, etc. (even in **swap**, the **a** is saying **o**). In other words, one grapheme can represent several phonemes:

the grapheme **y**   **my** ⎞
                              pretty ⎬ phonemes
                              year ⎠

- And to complicate things even more, most vowel phonemes can be represented by a number of different graphemes, for instance:

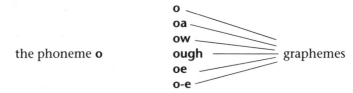

the phoneme **o**   **o**
                          oa
                          ow
                          ough ———— graphemes
                          oe
                          o-e

- The six basic vowels all have two sounds:
  - long (i.e. their alphabet names)
  - short (as in **cat**, **pet**, **pin**, **box**, **run**).

Strategies for the use of vowels in minimal phonic sampling

Children often take the injunction to 'build' a word quite literally, and set about laboriously building their way through the whole word. However, they need to know that phonics for reading means using a minimal phonic sample (as few letters as possible), which when put together with context will provide sufficient cues to know what the word is, for example 'The little boy was sc . . . of the dark'. So, as in supportive action 8, they need to be taught the useful strategy of phonically sampling the first bit of a word. In this, vowels will often prove the stumbling block.

The following strategies can be given to the learner to help him cope. He needs to know:

- where the first vowel is – even when unsure of its actual sound – in order to use onset as his minimal sample;
- that the consonant-onset alone may not be enough, and that a reader must dip into more than just the onset and take in the first vowel as part of the minimal sample. This is often so when the onset is just one consonant, for example Matthew's **labels** (see page 102).

This brings the reader up against the untrustworthy, complicated area of vowel behaviour:

- he should try the short sound of a basic single vowel before trying its long sound, because it is more likely to be short;
- he should nevertheless be willing to treat both long and short sounds as equally possible;
- he should not split a vowel digraph, for example **ra-in; r-ai-n** or **r-ain** would be acceptable;
- he needs to develop speed and flexibility of mind because minimal phonic sampling is all about juggling phonics and context.

8 An understanding of the role of syllables in word attack

A knowledge of syllables is important because, in the reading of multi-syllable words, it underpins the steps of the following process:

- the reader uses the first syllable (sometimes it takes the first two) to prompt a possible word from his receptive vocabulary;
- having generated a possible word, he returns to the page to map it against the print.

The more clearly he can recognize the auditory and the visual boundaries of syllables, the more easily he will match the possible word with the printed word.

TEXT: The pet rabbit came as a **disappointment** to the boys because they had really wanted an alligator.

BEN: *'The pet rabbit came as a di . . . a disappo.'* No. Wait a minute. I know **dis**. *Dis . . .* [pause] *disa* [pause] *disappo*

TEACHER: Hold on. Let's get these first two syllables sorted out. That's a good start. **Dis** is a very common syllable . . . it comes at the beginning of lots of words. Now see what else you think that **a** could be; vowels can have more than one sound, remember.

BEN: *Disapp . . .*

TEACHER: Good! You've sorted out the first two syllables. Now, did they want a rabbit? Read the whole sentence, just put your **disapp** in there . . .

BEN: *'The pet rabbit came as a disapp . . .'* Oh! they wanted an alligator. **Disappointment**!

TEXT: 'Are you just **pretending** to be ill?' asked Noddy.

BEN: *' "Are you just prĕt . . . end"'* [pauses]

TEACHER: Keep going.

BEN: *' "Are you just prĕt . . . end . . . to be ill . . .'*

TEACHER: Very close. You're so close you only need to make a little change. Remember: vowels can change their sounds. Show me the first vowel.

BEN: [points to the first **e**; pauses]

TEACHER: Don't forget another sound is **ē**. Go on. Try it.

BEN: *Prē . . . tend.* Ah! *' "Are you just* **prētending***"'*!

In these two episodes the teacher, in a one-to-one situation, was consolidating what had already been presented to Ben in whole-class work.

Syllable work is often thought of as a purely print activity, yet significant consolidation can be achieved through oral activities, devised to develop speed. This work can be delivered in brief sessions and needs very little preparation:

- putting syllables together to build whole words;
- generating as many words as possible from listening to a list of first syllables, or first two;
- thinking of a word after being given its definition and first syllable;
- completing a word embedded in a sentence, after being given its first syllable.

Child-friendly definitions of 'syllable' are rare, if non-existent, but thankfully, as with many other aspects of language, this does not prevent most children from grasping the concept. The two most important facts about syllables are:

- what a syllable is;
- where a syllable begins and ends.

In the absence of a good technical description suitable for children, the following working knowledge has been found to be dependable:

Syllables in spoken words – an intuitive recognition

- Syllables in spoken words seem to be intuitively recognized as 'beats' in a word.
- Children can be taught to clap beats or tap them out on the table/desk, or, while saying the word, to put the back of their hand under their chin and count the number of times their chin drops,
- or to place a finger along their lower lip and feel the number of times their mouth opens.

By first listening carefully to a multi-syllable word, followed by reading it on the board or OHP, a class can learn to match its spoken syllables with its written version. Each pupil then independently writes the word, underlining the syllables, or makes it with plastic letters, in separated syllables. (Underlining is preferable to using dividing lines, because it suggests the smoothness with which the word is to be rebuilt: **sat is fac tion** not **sat/is/fac/tion**.)

Such close analysis can be usefully transferred to the Look-Say-Cover-Write-Check spelling task (Peters and Smith 1993: 87), providing a focus for that first 'Look' section, so that **multiplication**, for example, is learned as five chunks, not 14 separate letters.

Syllables in written words – a learned recognition

Reliable information for word attack:

- A syllable may be a single vowel sound, or a single vowel sound plus the consonant(s) before it, after it, or on both sides of it (for example **I, no, it, well**).
- Syllables always have one vowel sound (**bed, bead, beard**).
- They can be complete words (**land, aid, sad**) or can be parts of words (**land-ing, aid-ed, sad-ly**).
- The vowel sound can be at the beginning or end of the syllable (**ex, pre**) or in the middle (**ment**).
- A closed syllable is one which is 'closed' when a consonant comes after the vowel (**ex, sad, ment**).
- A closed syllable usually has a short vowel sound.
- In words of more than one syllable where there are two consonants together, the boundary is between the two (**rab-bit, pic-nic, mid-ship-man**).

The following information is for flexible use in word attack – this is information often best understood *after* a word has been read!

- In words of more than one syllable where the syllable boundary is a single consonant the boundary is determined by whether the vowel is long or short (**no-tion, rob-in**).

- A short vowel will be in a closed syllable (**lem-on, hab-it, wag-on**).
- A long vowel is in an open syllable (**la-bel, pi-lot, no-tice**).

This information can only be effectively worked on via written words. First, pupils circle or highlight the vowel combinations (graphemes) in a multi-syllable word, then underline the syllables, taking note of syllable boundaries.

However, there is a danger of becoming too bound up in technicalities, and each teacher will need to decide how much technical knowledge will be of practical help to her children. An overemphasis on linguistic minutiae can be too much like focusing on the scratches on a window rather than on the wider view it affords. Although some knowledge of syllabification is helpful, some is far too complex for conscious application in the fluency which is essential to the reading process. Equally helpful is training in strategies of flexibility, most particularly in the question of vowel sounds. It was speedier and simpler to teach Ben to try out **prĕ** or **prē**, just as it was to teach Matthew **lă** or **lā** (supportive action 8, example 3) than to embroil them in detailed knowledge about language in mid-read. By teaching Ben to be flexible and to try out the two possibilities for the first vowel, his teacher had given him a workable reading strategy for coping with the complexity of syllable boundaries and their relationship with long or short vowels. He has a working tool to solve the problem. Discussion of the rules of syllabification can come at another time.

Prefixes and suffixes have meanings

If children are helped to see that prefixes and suffixes (affixes) have their own meanings, and that these change the root-words to which they are affixed, then their learning of phonics is once again being supported by meaning. Meanings make the affixes more memorable, so more likely to be automatically recognized as phonic elements. Furthermore, comprehension of that one part of the word improves comprehension of the whole. The list of prefixes is lengthy and useful (Beal 1991) but suffixes, apart from those referring to people (. . . **er**, . . . **or**, . . . **ant**, . . . **ee**) are usually less definable and more abstract (. . . **ious**, . . . **ment**).

9 An ability to make use of letter-string analogies between words

The code of our language repeats the same patterns in different words. Children need to develop a frame of mind in which they are ready to apply knowledge of a letter string learned in one word when meeting it in another:

> 'I've seen that before . . . That's in **train** (. . . **ain**). So this must be **sprain**';
> 'I know **ea** says **ĕă** in **head**, so this must be **threat**';
> or, even, (on meeting **psalm**): 'I know that the **p** at the beginning of **pterodactyl** doesn't say anything . . .'

A teacher can use the board or OHP for whole-class shared thinking about letter-string analogies, through:

- dividing one-syllable words into their onset and rime;
- generating lists of words sharing the same onset or the same rime, for example **str . . . ain**:

strain	**rain**
stroll	**train**
stride	**brain**
string	**Spain**
straight	**drain**

- preparing vocabulary for a forthcoming topic by presenting it in groups according to analogous letter strings.

  In introducing a topic about the timber industry, the teacher put two words on the board – **machine** and **chemicals** – and asked the children to think of other words using **ch** in similar ways.

ma*ch*ine	*ch*emicals
ma*ch*inery	s*ch*ool
avalan*ch*e	me*ch*anize
*ch*ute	me*ch*anization

(She also drew attention to **wood *ch*ip** and ***ch*ainsaw**).

The use of analogy as a reading strategy – the purpose of this work – must be kept to the fore, by showing children how to take a common letter string from a known word and use it to help generate an unknown word. For example, **cl** from ***cl*iff**, plus context, was used to generate ***cl*imber**.

'The *cl*imber *cl*everly *cl*imbed up the *cl*iff.' (**cliff**)

From such classwork, consolidation for groups and individuals may be provided through a range of games:

- matching games: basically, any card game which involves putting together onsets and rimes to make words. These can include nonsense words, provided the player can 'read' them.

  When words are collected as groups of 'known' and 'unknown', finding definitions for the 'unknown' pile extends vocabulary.

  And when players have to write these words, they can be trained to use the Look-Say-Cover-Write-Check technique as it was originally intended, focusing on relevant letter strings rather than on a sequence of separate letters, for example **ch-est** not **c.h.e.s.t.**, **thr-eat** not **t.h.r.e.a.t.**, and on meaning-based segments as well as syllables, for example **geo-logy**, **tele-vision**.
- recognition games, sometimes using whole words, sometimes letter strings, for example bingo, rummy and snap.

Letter-string analogy is an area of phonic knowledge which transfers particularly effectively from reading to writing, and vice versa.

10 An ability to sequence sounds smoothly (blending and building)

These traditional terms are often used interchangeably. However, they describe two separate processes. One (blending) works at the level of individual sounds. The other (building) works at the whole-word level:

> *blending* – the running-together of individual sounds: **s.n.** → **sn**, **s.p.r.** → **spr**, **ai.l.** → **ail**, **i.n.g.** → **i.ng**;
> *building* – the putting-together of larger chunks of sound: **sn.ail** → **snail**, **spr.int** → **sprint**; **sprint.ing** → **sprinting**.

Children usually develop an aptitude for blending and building if their early years were in classrooms where:

- there was extensive oral/aural experience of hearing words divided into meaningful groups of phonemes (blends and rimes), for example: 'I-Spy something beginning with **br** . . .' and Spoonerism games (see pages 37 and 46);
- their early introduction to written words followed the same principles, for example they met **c-at**, not **c.a.t.**, **fr-og**, not **f.r.o.g.** However, teachers must remain open-minded to those children who at first understand blending better if the word is 'topped' – as in **ca-t** – rather than 'tailed' – as in **c-at** (although the aim must be to move those children towards an appreciation of rime);
- the displays were of consonant blends and rimes rather than individual letters;
- playing with plastic letters was encouraged;
- computer games divided and rebuilt words;
- there were opportunities to make words with a variety of apparatus.

On earlier pages we have mentioned that consonant blends should be taught as wholes, and we have discussed the place of onset and rime practice, all of which is relevant here to this area of blending and building. So, to take the discussion a little further, we offer two suggestions which introduce meaning and interest to this area perhaps a little earlier than is sometimes the case:

- A child does not need to plough through all the single sounds before he can be introduced to blends; as soon as he has acquired even a handful of consonants he should be encouraged to make and use blends. It helps to teach the sounds of **l**, **r** and **s** as soon as possible, because with these he can construct all the blends as he steadily acquires the other consonants.
- Similarly, the concept of building should not be limited to the use of single-letter components – consonant-vowel-consonant words (c-v-c words). Children can begin building through putting together three kinds of components:
  - single letters
  - initial consonant blends
  - rimes.

Attaining smoothness in sequencing sounds in the building process

This is something to be developed to a large extent through demonstration. The following suggestions may help to make the teacher's task more effective:

- Whisper the sounds for blending, as this helps to eliminate the intrusive **uh** sound (schwa) which follows any consonant; the less it is voiced, the less intrusive it is.
- Show him how, instead of going pell-mell into building out loud, he should hold back from voicing anything while silently 'getting his mouth ready to':
  - shape it for the first consonant(s);
  - look ahead for the vowel or the whole rime, and *mentally* sound it;
  - go back then to the first consonant(s), having now got a view of the whole word.

  This will enable him to voice the first part, or the whole word, as one block of sound. He has looked at the onset, sampled the rime, gone back to say the onset, and then, having had a little thinking time, he is ready to put the two together – a more circular route than a single blinkered left-to-right progression.
- Demonstrate how to stretch a sound, continuing to voice it, while considering what the next sound may be **trrrrrr . . . ai-ai-ai-ai . . . pse**. This is better than cutting off each sound – **t.r.ai.p.se**.
- Provide children with mental images to help them visualize the blending and building processes. For example:
  - compare it to the blending of paint or the docking of two space ships;
  - mime onset and rime coming together by slowly bringing two hands together, interlocking fingers;
  - silently remind children about the process, as they read, by running a finger smoothly left–right under any appropriate word;
  - give children physical experience of building multi-syllable words, with plastic letters, or cards showing separate syllables.

11 An ability to recognize phonic elements at speed, developing automaticity

By 'phonic elements' we mean the 200 or so graphemes, plus rimes, affixes and syllables.

There should be an ever-present expectation in Assisted reading sessions for the reader to maintain a certain speed, in which the automatic recognition of phonic elements plays a key part.

Such swift recognition can be promoted through a range of games and activities, for instance:

- brief whole-class 'races', where lists of phonic elements and nonsense words are read against a stopwatch;

- quick-response games, in which phonic elements are read at speed after having been shown briefly on cards, or via OHP flashes;
- rummy and bingo, using phonic elements rather than whole words;
- timed multi-choice to complete a sentence: 'We mist/must/mast eat to live.'

Having a close link with spelling, this work may be usefully practised at appropriate levels with the different spelling groups within the class: while red group are dealing with vowel + consonant rimes (. . . **am**, . . . **et**, . . . **in**), and blue group with **ar, au, ai, or, ou** and **oi**, yellow group will be working with . . . **ious, bio** . . ., . . . **sion.**

12 An ability to talk about phonics using the correct terminology

Correct terms should be used from the outset, because correct terminology:

- helps to clarify the concepts;
- imposes some order on an otherwise unwieldy area;
- helps children to recognize phonics as a subject.

Each school, in the drawing up of its proactive spine, will need to decide on the technical terms it will include. The following list is not a teaching order, nor is it comprehensive, but it may serve as a starting point for such planning:

alphabet
a blend – a two-consonant blend
        – a triple/three-consonant blend
to blend
to build
capital letters and lowercase letters
consonant
digraph and trigraph
grapheme
morpheme
onset and rime
phoneme
prefix
rhyme
suffix
syllable
vowel, long and short.

All that has been discussed above regarding the teaching of the first two strands of phonic knowledge – facts and skills – aims to prevent three common mistakes:

- *phonic facts being taught without the necessary demonstration of their links to actual reading situations;*
- *phonic skills being presented in such a way that the overpowering message is: 'building is your sole recourse on meeting a problem word';*
- *a disproportionate amount of time being spent on phonic facts and building, an imbalance which leads the child to believe that 'Reading = phonic building'.*

The third strand of phonic knowledge, applied phonics, unifies facts and skills in real usage. It is as teachable as the other two strands.

APPLIED PHONICS – PUTTING PHONICS TO USE

Applied phonics brings balance to the overall provision of the teaching of phonics. It can be seen in use in every one of the Assisted reading episodes which illustrate the supportive actions, where the reader is constantly encouraged to move quickly to and fro between meaning and phonics, and the emphasis throughout is on fluency.

To make it work effectively, the following organization is essential:

- The child should feel that as much time is spent on applied phonics as on facts and skills, through:
  - whole-class demonstration of phonics in use
  - Assisted reading.
- Training about applied phonics is needed for all supporting adults.
- All supporting adults need to be kept informed about which phonic facts and skills a child is working on during the current term or half-term.
- There must be a system for the teacher to record both a child's good applications of phonics and his phonic needs, so that appropriate follow-up can take place. Information gathered from experienced helpers can be fed into this record system.
- By keeping his own record (see page 112) of some of the phonic facts discovered in the course of his Assisted reading, the pupil is constantly reminded of the reality and importance of applied phonics. Not everything which is met in a session will be recorded, only that which the adult suggests is relevant.

Finally, as we leave the topic of phonics, it is worth noting that however much we may analyse and classify the constituents of reading, there remains some other dimension. Earlier we made a comparison between reading and ski-ing. Now another analogy comes to mind:

A cricketer, pre-season, regularly goes through a set of routines to exercise those parts of his body relevant to his game. He works long and rigorously. However, after the first match of the season, despite all his preparation, he suffers unexpected aches and pains. What all his aching muscles tell him is that they have been used in ways that were *not* previously practised, because of the unique and unforeseeable combined demands of real play. The game had demanded something extra and quite different from all his preparatory exercises.

Implications for his future practice become clear:

- this extra element can only be improved by playing more games;
- however useful the separate skills' practices, they do not add up to the dimensions of real play;
- his skills' practice is not wasted, however, because it gives a strong foundation for his game;
- playing the game teaches him which skills he needs to practise separately.

CONCLUSION

This has been a chapter of finely detailed technical advice, but the last thing we would want is for a child to feel burdened by it. Part of the adult's task is to ensure that when the child walks away from an Assisted reading session he feels that he has had a good time, he has a clear idea about what he has learned, and he is motivated to come back because his efforts have been rewarded and enlightened by the quality of the praise he has received.

Chapter 5

Branching out

'Pupils read a range of texts fluently and accurately. They read independently, using strategies appropriately to establish meaning' (National Curriculum Level 3 description, DfEE 1995: 28). However, to make full use of that meaning they need a range of experiences interacting with a variety of texts.

Responsibility ratios 20 : 80 to 5 : 95

DEFINITION

Branching out, the last of our five stages, is a beginning, not an end. Although it is an end to intensive cueing strategy work, the reader is still only at the beginning of his lifetime's journey of reading.

Branching out starts with Level 3 of the National Curriculum, and we have taken one of the Level 3 descriptions as characteristic of this stage: 'Pupils read a range of texts fluently and accurately. They read independently, using strategies appropriately to establish meaning.'

However, the main work of this stage extends much further than reading the words; indeed, it goes further than the whole of the Level 3 description. We consider the goal is to bring the reader closer to realizing Ruth Strang's (1972: 68) vision: 'Reading provides experience through which the individual may expand his horizons; identify, extend and intensify his interests; and gain deeper understandings of himself, of other human beings, and of the world.' With this encompassing view, all of Levels 3–8 can be enhanced.

Branching out, therefore, requires the reader to:

- spend more time reading independently, receiving less assistance;
- attempt a more varied reading diet, exploring a range of genres;
- take part in a wider variety of activities, interacting with his reading;
- attempt some Instructional level text on his own.

HOW TO RECOGNIZE A CHILD READY FOR BRANCHING OUT: KEY CHARACTERISTICS

A child is ready for Branching out when:

- he can – 'fluently, accurately and independently' – read material at an approximate readability level of 10.0;
- the reader, on meeting a problem word, automatically and independently runs through the range of cueing tactics, predominantly with success;
- owing to his good level of cue use, the more he reads on his own the more he is able to teach himself about reading.

Readability level 10.0 is an important threshold. The degree of competence in Broad and Fine cueing strategies which such text requires is sufficient to prevent the reader from slipping back. Moreover, assuming he actually continues to read, it will cause him to make further progress independently, as he improves his use of the full range of cueing tactics, confirms and extends his automatic recognition of letter strings, and adds to his vocabulary. In fact, with support, skills adequate for readability level 10.0 can enable some secondary-school pupils to cope with their subject texts, despite those texts' having an average readability level of 12.0.

Readability

Up to now we have avoided discussion of objective measures of the difficulty level of any piece of reading material. Yet if 'reads fluently, accurately and independently' is to make sense we have to ask: 'reads *what* fluently, accurately and independently?' For instance, a Bookbinding child may read the simple captions to the picture story *Rosie's Walk* fluently, accurately and independently ('through the gate . . . over the fence . . .'), but this in no way qualifies him for Branching out – hence our introduction now of a more specific readability guideline.

Numerical gradings of the difficulty level of reading materials are the outcome of readability measures. Language is too complex to be adequately represented by numbers, but quantitative measures can form a useful part of a teacher's range of assessment methods. However, it should be remembered that:

- readability formulae can only measure Reading the lines, not Between and Beyond;
- the findings of any formula are governed by whatever features its author considered important to measure – the most usual being word length, sentence length and number of frequently used words – and so different outcomes are produced from formula to formula.

We include one straightforward example: Fry's readability graph (Fry 1968: 513–16, 575–8) (Figure 5.1).

Figure 5.1   **Fry's readability graph**

In selecting material for pupils, a guide to its readability level may prove helpful.

Method

1 Select three separate 100-word passages, preferably from the beginning, middle and end of the material.
2 In each passage find:
   – the total number of syllables
   – the total number of sentences.
3 Find the average number of syllables and sentences for all three passages.
4 Read off on the graph below. The nearer to the black line, the more accurate the figure.

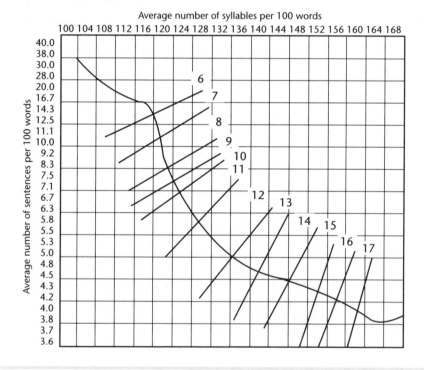

THE BASIC COMPONENTS OF READING: READING THE LINES, READING BETWEEN THE LINES, READING BEYOND THE LINES

Although the reader has now arrived at the point where he is competent in the skills of one component of reading (cueing strategies), he does need further skills to become fully adept in the other components.

A list of such skills appears in the National Curriculum (Figure 5.2).

Figure 5.2   **National Curriculum Reading Level descriptions 3–8**

Level 3

- Pupils read a range of texts fluently and accurately.
- They read independently, using strategies appropriately to establish meaning.
- In responding to fiction and non-fiction they show understanding of the main points and express preferences.
- They use their knowledge of the alphabet to locate books and find information.

Level 4

- In responding to a range of texts, pupils show understanding of significant ideas, themes, events and characters, beginning to use inference and deduction.
- They refer to the text when explaining their views.
- They locate and use ideas and information.

Level 5

- Pupils show understanding of a range of texts, selecting essential points, and using inference and deduction where appropriate.
- In their responses, they identify key features, themes and characters, and select sentences, phrases and relevant information to support their view.
- They retrieve and collate information from a range of sources.

Level 6

- In reading and discussing a range of texts, pupils identify different layers of meaning and comment on their significance and effect.
- They give personal responses to literary texts, referring to aspects of language, structure and themes in justifying their views.
- They summarize a range of information from different sources.

Level 7

- Pupils show understanding of the ways in which meaning and information are conveyed in a range of texts.
- They articulate personal and critical responses to poems, plays and novels, showing awareness of their thematic, structural and linguistic features.
- They select and synthesize a range of information from a variety of sources.

As the standard blueprint from which teachers must work, it provides a helpful skill-by-skill account of what readers must do. However, it would be regrettable if it were to be their only recourse. This would be to neglect the wealth of knowledge and experience accumulated over the last century.

If it were to become teachers' sole port of call, it could leave them with:

- an incomplete model of reading, with no clear indication that there are permanent components – the basics;
- a difficult task in separating skill from component, as it drifts from one to the other: 'In responding . . . pupils show understanding . . . of the main points . . .' (How much 'understanding', I wonder? What exactly constitutes a 'response'?);
- a cumulative, linear view of reading development, leading to piece-meal planning ('I don't need to worry about inference and deduction at Level 2 – they don't come in until Level 4').

However, a different perspective is possible. By regrouping that serial list, its descriptions can be categorized as the components of reading.

This perspective is illustrated in Figures 5.3 and 5.4, to reflect the basics which underpin work at all five developmental stages:

- reading the lines;
- reading Between the lines;
- reading Beyond the lines (see Figure R.1).

Finding and selecting, and using evidence – the two components shown here for the first time – support those three permanent components.

By reconsidering the National Curriculum in this way, teachers can benefit from:

- a clearer understanding
  - of each description;
  - of the component into which each fits;
  - of all parts of the model, descriptions and components, as insepara-ble and interdependent;
- a better-informed structure to underpin planning.

SUGGESTIONS FOR PRACTICE

It is precisely because the components of reading are interdependent that we choose not to separate them when organizing classroom work. To do so would distort reading. Instead, we suggest four types of work:

- reading interviews;
- reading experience at the three levels;
- activities to develop 'knowledge about reading' (Kingman 1988);
- DARTs (Directed Activities in Reading and Thinking).

To complete any activity in these four areas, the reader uses several of the components of reading, sometimes all five. This is the nature of read-ing.

**National Curriculum Reading Level descriptions regrouped as the basics
(Level numbers in brackets)**
note that some descriptions fit more than one component

Finding and selecting
- Pupils use their knowledge of the alphabet to locate books and find information. (3)
- They locate and use ideas and information. (4)
- They retrieve and collate information from a range of sources. (5)
- They summarize a range of information from different sources. (6)
- They select and synthesize a range of information from a variety of sources. (7)

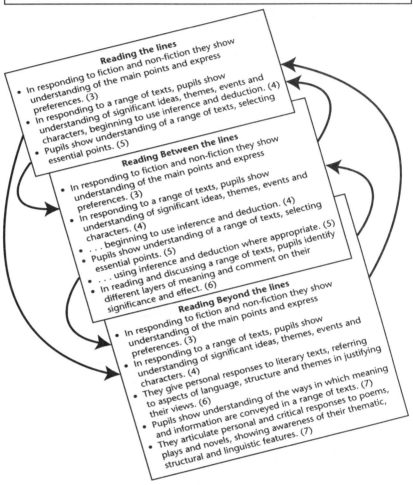

Reading the lines
- In responding to fiction and non-fiction they show understanding of the main points and express preferences. (3)
- In responding to a range of texts, pupils show understanding of significant ideas, themes, events and characters, beginning to use inference and deduction. (4)
- Pupils show understanding of a range of texts, selecting essential points. (5)

Reading Between the lines
- In responding to fiction and non-fiction they show understanding of the main points and express preferences. (3)
- In responding to a range of texts, pupils show understanding of significant ideas, themes, events and characters. (4)
- . . . beginning to use inference and deduction. (4)
- Pupils show understanding of a range of texts, selecting essential points. (5)
- . . . using inference and deduction where appropriate. (5)
- In reading and discussing a range of texts, pupils identify different layers of meaning and comment on their significance and effect. (6)

Reading Beyond the lines
- In responding to fiction and non-fiction they show understanding of the main points and express preferences. (3)
- In responding to a range of texts, pupils show understanding of significant ideas, themes, events and characters. (4)
- They give personal responses to literary texts, referring to aspects of language, structure and themes in justifying their views. (6)
- Pupils show understanding of the ways in which meaning and information are conveyed in a range of texts. (7)
- They articulate personal and critical responses to poems, plays and novels, showing awareness of their thematic, structural and linguistic features. (7)

Using evidence
- They refer to the text when explaining their views. (4)
- In their responses, they identify key features, themes and characters, and select sentences, phrases and relevant information to support their view. (5)
- They give personal responses to literary texts, referring to aspects of language, structure and themes in justifying their views. (6)
- Pupils show understanding of the ways in which meaning and information are conveyed in a range of texts. (7)
- They articulate personal and critical responses to poems, plays and novels, showing awareness of their thematic, structural and linguistic features. (7)

Figure 5.4   Components of accomplished reading: the basic model revisited

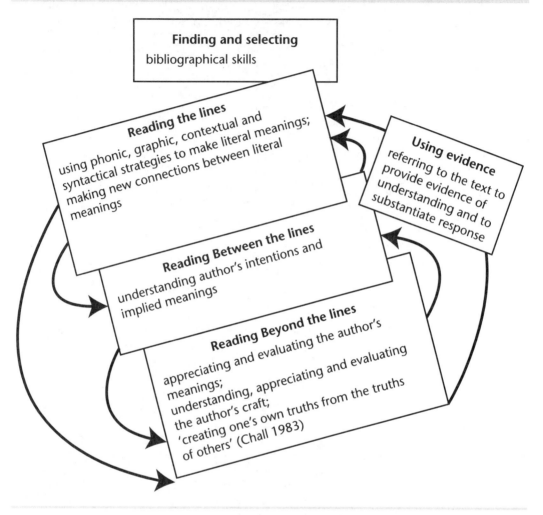

These four types of work comprise a recipe, and the ingredients may be mixed according to need. The amounts may vary at different times and for different pupils, and include individual, group and whole-class work.

Reading interviews

As we have emphasized, there is no sharp dividing line between the end of any stage and the beginning of the next. Certainly there is considerable overlap between Assisted reading and Branching out, and a child at the beginning of this stage may still require Assisted reading support for some Instructional level text (see the initial responsibility ratio).

However, once a child's cueing strategies are well established, and Assisted reading sessions quite phased out, Reading interviews provide continuing opportunity for one-to-one time.

Figure 5.5	Reading interviews

The aims of a Reading interview are:

- to let the child know that you are still interested in his reading, even though Assisted reading sessions no longer form part of his tuition;
- to monitor his progress in the reading skills of the Branching out stage;
- to monitor the range and balance of his reading;
- to supply fresh direction to his development when necessary.

The frequency and duration of a Reading interview:

- once or perhaps twice a term, for about ten minutes; the pupil is given advance notice.

What goes on in a Reading interview (a menu):

- teacher and pupil discuss the range of books on his record;
- teacher and pupil discuss one book, including Between and Beyond its lines;
- pupil explains his preferences and dislikes;
- pupil explains why he has chosen certain passages to show his teacher, for example: they puzzle him; they were exciting, funny, sad, etc.; he wishes he had written them (this is a way of getting the pupil to look at the craft of the writer);
- pupil reads a passage – his choice or teacher's. It may be unprepared, unlike Assisted reading, provided the pupil feels comfortable and sees the usefulness;
- teacher sets questions requiring scanning and searching;
- teacher summarizes pupil's progress with him, and sets new target(s).

How the pupil should prepare for the interview:

- knowing the format, he will have ready
  - his reading record
  - his current reading
  - one or two of the books on his reading record
  - any other reading;
- knowing that he is going to be asked to point out certain passages, he should make use of bookmarks.

Reading experiences at the three levels

Frustration level (10 or more problem words per 100 words)

It is important that pupils continue to have Frustration level text read to them, for all the reasons first stated in Assisted reading (see page 71).

There is another way to approach Frustration level material, which is to provide individual support through the technique of Paired reading.

Paired reading is a technique where adult and pupil read aloud, almost in unison, at a natural pace. The adult takes the lead, as the pupil keeps up, both saying every word out loud. The pupil or adult points to the words being read out, the finger moving smoothly across the page. It is best if the pupil points: it maintains his concentration, and the adult can take her lead from him, matching her reading speed to the pace of the finger.

Because the texts are at Frustration or even high Instructional level, the reader can choose material which interests him, which may well be non-fiction.

Paired reading enables the pupil to partake in a good model of reading. Hearing book language at speed familiarizes him with an extensive range of its conventions. This helps with well-known stumbling blocks, including:

- literary turns of phrase ('Long had they yearned for a child . . .');
- dialogue (for example sometimes there is no indication of who is speaking, or it comes after the speech);
- colloquialisms (**ugh**! **geroff**!);
- contractions (**we'll**, etc.).
- many features common to information text (for example passive verbs: 'The herds were preyed on by . . .'; or a noun clause as subject: 'What lies beneath the surface is a mystery').

Vocabulary is extended; the ability to predict improves. The list could go on, and indeed the fact that it is so lengthy is one of the great advantages of the technique.

However, the benefits reach further than language, to include an improved self-image:

- the child is allowed to be an equal in the reading partnership;
- he is never allowed to fail;
- he is freed from the tension of mistake-ridden practice;
- he is set free to choose what he reads;
- he is given confidence and helped to build self-esteem.

Although often thought of as a purely restorative technique to be introduced when a child needs fresh impetus to rescue his reading development, Paired reading has a wider application. There are reluctant readers whose development is normal, but who, because of their lack of interest, are *not* going to be the self-teaching type who learn to read by reading. Their reading will stay at around readability level 9.0 unless their attitude towards it can be revitalized. Paired reading can lift them through the important threshold of Branching out.

It has been found that Paired reading for 15 minutes every day for six weeks improves some children's reading by up to 18 months.

Finally, it can be the means of repairing fractured reading relationships between parent and child, as both learn a new technique together. What is more, they rediscover that relaxing and having fun need not impair progress.

Instructional level (technically 3–10 word recognition problems per 100 words. Here at this stage, it is best at 5–6 per 100)

As we have said, a key characteristic of this stage is the self-teaching inherent in 'learning to read by reading', in which progress comes from the successful independent tackling of difficult words.

This is why a reader now should be expected to take up the challenge of Instructional level, in increasing amounts, and – crucially – with less support. Further benefits will include increased general reading confidence and reading stamina.

However, it does need to be remembered that at the far end of Instructional level lies Frustration level. Those benefits accruing from tackling Instructional level text are best attained from somewhere in the middle of that band – perhaps no more than five or six problem words per 100.

Moreover, there must be a support system, with a clear expectation that it will be used. By continuing to apply traffic light self-monitoring methods, pupils will recognize when their reading is at Instructional level, and so know to seek support whenever their own efforts are not enough. They need to know where to go for help, and that may be classroom helper, reading partner, dictionary or glossary. For selected texts there may be recorded help (résumé or background information, in print or recorded on cassette or Language Master: see page 85).

There is also another branch of support which always proves helpful: that of giving a reader a clear purpose for reading, and perhaps how he should follow it up.

Finally, it is important that the challenges of Instructional level are worked on collaboratively within group and whole-class sessions.

Independent level (0–3 word recognition problems per 100 words)

- Pupils should still be using the traffic light system to choose books at their Independent level. Teachers need to ensure that pupils are doing so:
  - in Reading interviews
  - through whole-class instruction
  - through spot-checks.
- The range should include:
  - a balance of fact and fiction
  - a wide range of prose and poetry
  - a wide variety of genres and registers.
- Pupils should be motivated to read by:
  - attractive and accessible library corners in classrooms
  - books visible and available around the classroom
  - attractive and accessible libraries
  - book weeks; book fairs; book swaps
  - introduction to authors via displays, posters etc.

- authors invited for workshops (for teachers and parents as well as for pupils)
- 'taster' readings in assemblies and in class.
- Pupils should have opportunity for, and training in, sustained independent reading, building on the principles of Uninterrupted Sustained Silent Reading (USSR):
  - reading is sufficiently important to be given prime time
  - the pupils' own reading instructors should practise what they preach.
- In pupils' responses to their reading:
  - their own records should go beyond date of start and finish to include pupils' evaluation of each book: this can be as simple as star-ratings 1 to 5
  - their reflections during reading should include *oral*, informal commentary made to an adult during the course of a book, perhaps three times per book, or at some chapter-ends. Comments can be impressions, predictions, reactions, and links to own experience. Their *written journals* share the same aims as the oral reflections. Pupils must feel secure that, as purely personal comments, their thoughts are not destined for a wide audience. Some children will prefer to remain with oral commentaries, others will find oral experience prepares them for keeping a written journal
  - there should be class records of books read, with evaluations, for example a 'bookworm': children put brief details of a book with an evaluative comment, onto separate circular cards; these are then wall-mounted, cumulatively, in the form of a segmented 'worm'
  - ideas to help teachers are given in Figure 5.6.

Knowledge about reading

The following activities lend themselves quite comfortably to whole-class sessions of approximately 15 minutes:

- practice in pupils' self-monitoring of their own three reading levels (see page 78);
- whole class sharing word attack (see page 115);
- practice in 'gap completion' (see pages 145 and 147, under DARTs);
- rehearsing and giving 'reading performances';
- spot-checks on star-ratings from pupils' reading records (see above);
- word histories: continuing the exploration of word derivations begun in Assisted reading (see page 114);
- register break puzzles: pupils are asked to find the one phrase or sentence, written by the teacher and inserted into a short extract from elsewhere, which is in a register completely out of character with the rest of the passage;
- creating root webs, for knowledge of word meanings, letter-string familiarization and spelling, for example this one from Ramsden (1993: 24):

Figure 5.6	Responses after reading

1 Your favourite character in the story comes to your home. What happens?
2 Write and illustrate the noises that were in your story.
3 What birthday gift would you give each character in your story? Why?
4 Make up a 'missing person' poster for a person in the book.
5 Make up a 'lost or found' advertisement for an object in your book.
6 You can look into the future: what happened to your favourite character after the book came to an end?
7 Make up an invitation for a friend to read the book you have just finished.
8 Fold a piece of paper in half. Draw where the story was set on one side. Draw where you live on the other side.
9 Write a newspaper article about something that happened in the story. Make the headlines suit your newspaper.
10 Design costumes for the characters in your book.
11 Design a book cover illustrating your favourite character.
12 Make a photograph album. Draw photographs of the characters in the story.
13 Make a zig-zag book from a strip of paper. Make a comic strip about the book you have read.
14 Make a day's diary for a character in your story.
15 Draw a map of any journey in the book.
16 Be in the story as yourself, in place of one of the characters. How does that change what happens?

Root-web

resign	signature	consign
resignation	signatory	consignment
resigning		consigned

sign

assign		design
assignment		designer
assignation		designing
reassign	signal	designed
	signalled	designation
	signalling	designate
		redesign

- 'three-speed reading' (see Figure 5.7)
- bibliographical knowledge
  - at book level: contents, index, glossary, preface, introduction, blurb, date of publication, captions, sub-headings, italics, bold, capitals and underlining for emphasis
  - at library level: catalogues and classification numbers;
- dictionary skills;
- thesaurus skills.

Figure 5.7   Three-speed reading

Scan: looking for facts
Often for this kind of reading the answer will be just one word. Often the scanning will be in directories, dictionaries, encyclopaedias and the indices of books.

Typically the reader asks: When? Who? Where? Which? What?

Search
looking for reasons, causes, comparisons, steps and stages.

Typically the reader asks: How? Why?

Deep-read
in order to form judgements, to appreciate, to enjoy

DARTs

'DART' stands for Directed Activity in Reading and Thinking (or Directed Activity Related to Text). DARTs are wide ranging and powerful allies in a teacher's resolve to lead young readers to read Between and Beyond the lines. Wherever reading occurs in the curriculum, DARTs draw pupils painlessly into making fuller meaning from it.

A DART requires pupils to work on a piece of reading as they read it for the first time. *It is not work done after reading.*

It is a game-like activity which by its very nature leads pupils to pause and reflect. *It is not passive; it is not copying out.*

It is worked on by pupils in pairs or small groups. *It is not work which isolates.*

It requires collaborative talk between pupils. *It is not silent work.*

It is applied to reading material which forms part of the curriculum. *It is not exercise for its own sake.*

It is usually open-ended, with no set 'right' answer. *It is not work which demoralizes.*

There are two types of DART:

- DARTs which reconstruct the passage;
- DARTs which analyse the passage.

The activities which comprise these two types of DART are detailed on the DARTboard (Figure 5.8).

Figure 5.9 adds further detail to one section of the DARTboard, 'Creative follow-ups'.

Figure 5.8   The DARTboard

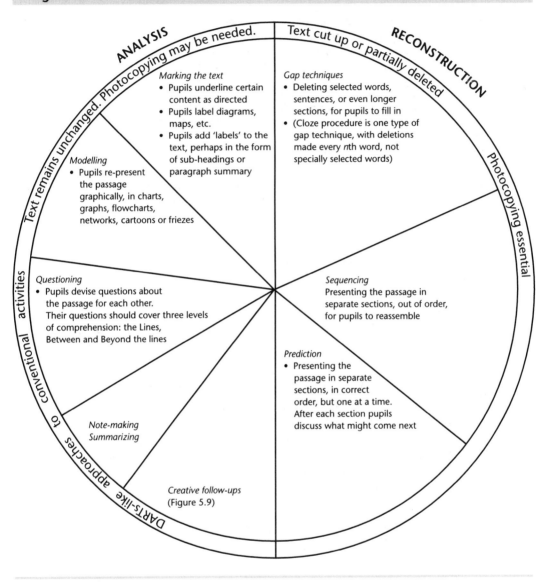

Figure 5.9	Creative follow-ups		
Modelling Presenting the content as picture or diagram; words may or may not be included	**Changing the form** Presenting the content but in a different form	**Parallel production** Presenting fresh ideas parallel to the original content	**Being a critic** Making objective yet entertaining evaluations
Realistic illustration of the text (scenes, characters, events), perhaps with quotations	Dramatic reading with, for example choral speaking, dialogue, sound effects	Present the 'before' of a story, poem, etc.	Review the book for a newspaper
Atmospheric illustrations/artwork capturing the mood (perhaps for a book jacket)	Dance presentation	Present a spin-off from a story, poem, etc.	Write the 'blurb' for the book's jacket
Episodic work, for example a frieze	Slide presentation	Put a character from the book into another context	Write to the author, or to a friend, about the book
Map of a journey	Write as film scenario	Produce a scrapbook which a character might have produced, on material outside the book	Teacher or pupil role-plays the author and is interviewed
Drawings or plans of buildings	Imagine you are a character in the book. Tell the story from that point of view	Relive in your own circumstances events similar to those in the book	Stage a pretend TV or radio chat show, and discuss the book
An excerpt summarized in cartoon form (encourage use of thought bubbles)	Meet a character and question him/her about his/her actions	Use the style of a poem, description, etc. to write something new	From five named books, claim that one must be destroyed. Debate which it should be
Family trees	Several characters discuss events from the book		Collections of excerpts – long or short – wall mounted with reasons for their selection
Depict the good and evil in the book in some format decided by pupils	Plan the break-off points for a serialization of the book		Choice of ten 'Desert Island' poems/books/ characters, etc.
Wallchart of significant quotations to represent a chapter, character or theme (groups may adopt one each)			

DARTs possess great power and versatility:

- DARTs engage pupils, in the course of a single task, in talking about both subject-content and language issues:

  > A group of readers were filling the gap left by omitting **exact** from this sentence: 'William demanded an [exact] number of knights from each of his nobles depending on the size and value of their lands.' Their teacher had omitted **exact** to focus on the relationship between what the king gave and what he demanded.

  By chance, the pupils had to juggle a language fact (that an initial vowel must follow **an**) with a historical fact, and in this instance, it was the language fact which clinched their historical understanding.

- DARTs need not always take up planning time:

  > words hidden by Blu-tack can produce an instant gap activity, or a grid can be quickly sketched on the board to prompt analysis. In the poem 'Hurt no living thing' the meanings of lines such as 'moth with dusty wing' and 'grasshopper so light of leap' were explored through putting into one column of the grid how each insect moved, and in another what it looked like.

- DARTs should be treated flexibly, avoiding any routine association of one activity with one type of text. For example, prediction is as fruitful with information text as with fiction, as effective at sentence level as at text level:

  > Thinking about criteria for town-siting, a group of pupils were asked to predict phrase by phrase what ideas might follow breaks within sentences: ' Within a town industries are attracted to sites which . . .'

- DARTs allow pupils to go Beyond the lines into concerns which may have remained uncovered had the work been completely teacher-driven:

  > Several groups were working to sequence the separated lines of Gavin Ewart's poem 'Arithmetic', describing the burdensome routine of one schoolchild in caring for younger siblings, and consequent misunderstandings in school. One group's disagreement about whether the anonymous carer is girl or boy became a whole-class debate about gender issues, none of which were overtly raised by the lines themselves.

Figure 5.10 illustrates the relationship of the various DARTs to the three components of our basic reading model.

Figure 5.10   DARTs and the basic reading model

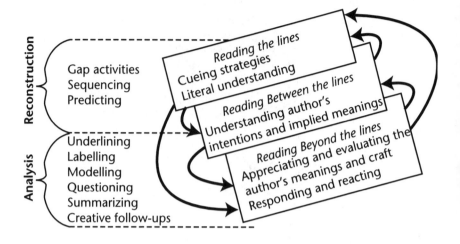

Figure 5.11   Practical steps in preparing a DART

1 Identify a suitable passage, with
   - content which is important to your curriculum
   - a reading level which is Instructional for the majority within each group (3–10 problem words per 100 words).
2 Consider which aspect of the content you wish to focus on.
3 Consider the structure of the passage. Is it a sequence of events, is it cause-and-effect, does it tell of the structure of something, is it a description in which adjectives are important, etc.?
4 Use your decisions from 2 and 3 to help you select the specific DART. For instance, a sequence of events suggests sequencing or prediction; a structure might lend itself to labelling a diagram; interesting discussion will come from deleting adjectives from a description; cause-and-effect may well be depicted in a table.
5 Think how to present the materials. In what form will you actually hand it to your pupils? Can you make it reusable, to offset some of your time used on its preparation. Consider acetate overlays for DARTs which call for marking the text.
6 Check the copyright guidelines for any material you reproduce.
7 Consider your classroom organization. Possibilities include:
   - only one group working on a DART; if the rest of the class can be differently occupied with comparatively independent tasks, this allows the teacher to take part, but beware of trying to lead or sway the group too much
   - pyramid-planning: the children discuss in pairs, and reach an agreement; the pairs join up to form fours, and they too must reach a consensus; finally, all join in whole-class discussion

    – class in groups, each working on the same DART; a spokesperson from
      each group reports back to the whole class; this may lead to further
      work.
8 Introducing DARTs:
    – consider what preparation of pupils – and staff – might be needed
      because of DARTs' wide use of discussion
    – pupils will need training and practice in the techniques of DARTs
      before working on them independently.

CONCLUSION

We have chosen to leave the developing reader at this stage, but he is not
at the end of learning to read. Rather, he is about to embark on a continuing journey, and it is one for which he is now well equipped.
Although his texts may become increasingly challenging, those self-
same 'basics' to which he was introduced in Bookbinding will carry on
serving him well as he continues to branch out to new authors, new
experiences, new worlds.

Chapter 6

The team approach – teachers, parents and helpers

Throughout his journey towards independent reading, a child must experience a comprehensive range of literacy activities. He needs to hear text at his Frustration and Instructional levels, as well as having plenty of reading practice at his Independent level. He needs the opportunity to respond individually to what he has read, and time to browse and choose. He needs time to interact with a text with others in a group. He needs tuition and practice in specific skills at text, sentence and word level. He needs to have the integrated use of cues demonstrated.

All these are vital.

The arrival of the Literacy Hour, therefore, is heartening for it will have the power to set children in front of print in a determined and systematic way. This elevation of literacy is something which reading teachers throughout Britain have been recommending for years, but without the necessary authority. If this welcome initiative succeeds – for it is a magnificent experiment apparently as yet unproven by any substantial research – it will be for reasons long advocated by literacy teachers:

- reading will have been promoted as a subject in its own right, with the curriculum rearranged to accommodate it;
- teachers, parents and children will all have been made aware of the importance of reading;
- children will have been given safeguarded opportunities to read more;
- the potency of peer-group interaction will have been utilized;
- children will have received effective tuition in the whole range of skills involved in reading.

However, because this initiative relies entirely on class and group teaching, a note of caution should be sounded. Historically, attractive new moves in education have sometimes entailed the throwing-out of the baby with the bathwater, and one-to-one reading support may be in danger of being one such baby. But it carries such advantages that it must not be jettisoned. Its irreplaceable contribution must complement whatever other raft of provision also exists.

THE VALUE OF ONE-TO-ONE WORK

There are three areas of strength which only one-to-one can add to the total reading programme:

- *The child's learning benefits from receiving immediate tailored feedback.* Just as no two readers ever approach the same page in quite the same way, so there is a huge variety in text itself – each page is always different from any other. To help children accommodate to this range of permutations, one-to-one delivers personally appropriate support at the precise point of individual need. Moreover, it is able to sustain this intensively over a complete passage.

    There is a particular rigour inherent in one-to-one which can be delivered in no other way.
- *The quality of observation on offer is uniquely illuminating.* This essential area was discussed earlier in the Rationale chapter. We would like to extend those comments here by making a legitimate comparison with learning to write. A child's written work receives one-to-one attention whenever it is marked, and this amounts to a considerable number of hours over his school life. From this investment his teachers keep themselves up to date about his learning needs. In fact, under this guise one-to-one is fully accepted in most aspects of the curriculum. Reading, although lacking visible product, surely deserves a similar expenditure of time.
- *The teacher taps into a rich vein of professional insights.* Supporting children's reading development by working with them one-to-one provides such a wealth of insights into the process of reading that it constitutes a constant refresher course. Without regular close exposure to these real demonstrations of the bare bones of children's problem-solving, there is a tendency to become over-theoretical. For the teacher new to reading support, one-to-one provides a necessary increase of knowledge to deploy in groupwork, and for the experienced teacher it maintains the freshness and realism groupwork demands. It keeps awareness alive, and is a source of informative events, some of which can profitably be shared with class and group. Class and group teaching without the genuine understanding and inspiration which comes from regular one-to-one would be rather like painting by numbers.

ORGANIZATION FOR THE PROVISION OF ONE-TO-ONE SUPPORT

The unique value of one-to-one tuition, then, is not something to be squeezed out by pressure of time. It is of such priority that organizational solutions must be found. If these can be instituted they will act as preventative measures, avoiding the consequent layers of emotional and, possibly, behavioural problems. For if children experience prolonged struggle and failure the school will eventually be presented with the even greater organizational task of providing remediation. More effective, both educationally and financially, is the early provision of skilled, focused one-to-one work.

As we have indicated, for their own and their pupils' benefit, class teachers themselves need to provide some of this. But it is quite clear that they cannot provide all, and the only way is to work cooperatively, through a team approach. Four teams are possible, maybe more than one working at the same time:

- class teacher and paid helpers;
- class teacher and volunteer helpers;
- class teacher and one or more members of the child's family;
- class teacher and other children as helpers.

The teaching of reading demands the expertise of professional teachers, so of course it is they who direct each team's work. Furthermore, helpers and parents cannot be effective without proper training – a fact which, although given heightened importance by the advent of the Literacy Hour, should receive permanent recognition.

The remainder of this chapter considers the groundwork needed for the successful implementation of the team approach, through:

- a helper system:
  - recognition of need
  - a steady start
  - the school's reading policy
  - voluntary help: issues, recruitment, contract and training;
- the home–school partnership
  - parents' meetings.

A HELPER SYSTEM

Recognition of need

The team approach must stem from a united staff perception of a need for improvement in the quality of their school's reading support. It may be that the requirements of the Special Educational Needs Code of Practice have brought to light the number of children with unexpectedly low reading levels, or it may be that new staff have questioned overall levels of expectation. The needs of individual schools differ, and each school will need to decide which single one of the four teams will initially yield the most benefits. For example:

School A, under a new head, has just embarked on an expansion of its total reading support. It already has three paid classroom assistants, only one of whom is trained for literacy work, and seven volunteer helpers, all untrained. So, a priority for this school is to train all ten together.

School B has three paid classroom assistants and no volunteer helpers. The classroom assistants are not specifically trained in literacy development, and are allocated to six teachers who are using them for general classroom help. A school which confines its paid helpers to practical chores may not be getting best value for money. If it replaces the general classroom help with volunteer help, no single teacher need feel any loss. Then its priority can be to train the three paid helpers for reading support and to focus their help on children with literacy needs.

School C has two paid helpers trained and experienced in supporting reading. However, it also has a number of volunteer helpers, inconsistent in attendance, enthusiastic but untrained. Each employs her own personal brand of support, and a glance round the school reveals all kinds of methods going on at once. This school needs to consider carefully the quality and deployment of its volunteers. Next, through training all the helpers, a unified approach can be ensured.

A steady start

What any school needs to keep firmly in mind if it is to build a helper system, with all its invaluable benefits, is the considerable time and energy required to set it up. Such projects must be done well, or left alone: better a small scale initiative undertaken by one class teacher than an overambitious whole-school scheme which may be difficult to organize and maintain. Therefore:

- It is important never to reach out beyond what can be managed at any one time.
- Start from where you are and grow from there.
- Avoid the temptation to try to help as many current pupils as possible.
- Ensure one project is securely in place before embarking on the next.
- Untrained or hastily trained helpers are not the answer.
- A more thorough training gives helpers the necessary support and experience of success.
- Quality of training has a dual outcome:
  - more children are appropriately supported long-term,
  - helpers develop a loyalty to the school. (The resulting stability can only enhance the school's reputation.)

The school's reading policy

As we have said, from a staff's recognition of the school's reading needs, a combined effort can produce a set of goals, and ways and means of attaining those goals.

In framing its policy, a school should be concerned to ensure that:

- reading development is everyone's responsibility and not confined to one individual, for example special needs coordinator or Language/literacy postholder;
- there is a consistent methodology for the teaching of reading;
- a high priority is placed on reading, both at school and at home;
- school and home equally value each other's role;
- there are high expectations of reading achievement;
- a significant proportion of paid helpers' time is devoted to literacy;
- there is a commitment to training sessions for parents;
- there is one consistent framework with written guidelines for training helpers and parents;
- there are guidelines for recruiting volunteer helpers;
- there is an informal contract covering the role of volunteer helpers;
- the policy is revisited regularly to maintain it as a working document.

Professional sharing is an important element for the success of a policy. If literacy issues are seen as everybody's concern, all will be encouraged to be open about what has worked for them and where they need help. While one teacher may feel able to coordinate one of the teams, perhaps her own helper team, she may feel unsure about setting up a larger system, the school-parents team perhaps. If all can feel comfortable in drawing on the support and experience of each other, the pool of expertise will grow.

Volunteer helpers in school

Issues

The introduction of this topic often raises concerns, not least of which is the question of its long-term effect. Some regard that positively: more children can be helped. Others, although acknowledging it as well-meaning, regard it as merely shoring up deficiencies in the central funding of professional teachers.

However, many schools use volunteer helpers with success, finding that the benefits far outweigh any potential difficulties. Admittedly, some volunteers are transitory, as the qualities they must bring to reading support – being literate, organized, sympathetic and communicative – often take them into paid employment. Yet their literacy support skills are rarely wasted. They remain with them to be deployed in their extended families, workplaces, and other voluntary work, thereby adding to the school's reputation as a community resource.

The comparative table (Figure 6.1) may help the debate.

Figure 6.1	Volunteer helpers in schools: benefits and considerations

Benefits	Considerations
Creates opportunity for more one-to-one work	Can be perceived as a threat to professionalism
Children realize that parents are supporting the school and its values	Requires substantial investment of time for initial training
Parents reassured by school's open sharing of teaching methods	Regular monitoring has time implications
Raises profile of literacy in school and community	Potential for breaches of confidentiality
Realities of school life more widely understood, promoting increased parental support	Volunteers may be unable to sustain their involvement
Creates a pool of trained helpers for possible future employment (for example as classroom assistant or statemented special needs support)	

Recruitment

High-profile mass recruitment drives can lead to difficulties. A safer alternative (also check local education authority guidelines for any police vetting requirements) is to consult staff on the suitability of available potential volunteers: parents, grandparents, governors and members of the local community. A helpful way in is to invite these candidates to assist with practical tasks in the classroom, in situations in which they can be observed interacting with children. Thus insights may be gained into their working styles before inviting them to help with reading. This puts the teachers in the driving seat from the beginning.

Once invited, build in a six-week trial and a get-out clause for either side. This acts as a further safety measure, ensuring that neither party is offended nor obligated.

Contract

An informal contract, included in the school policy, contributes to the success of the scheme by giving it deserved recognition. The school benefits from volunteers, so it should offer benefits to them. The contract should include the reciprocal requirements shown in Figure 6.2.

Figure 6.2   Volunteer helpers' contract

The school requires a professional attitude from the volunteers:

- an open mind (a willingness to adopt the school's methods without clouding the issue with preconceived ideas);
- consistency of attendance (the same weekly time(s); notification when unable to come in);
- commitment to a reasonable minimum timespan (six months to a year);
- confidentiality (non-committal responses to outside quizzing);
- record-keeping (a notebook which stays in school, with pupils recorded under first names only).

The volunteers require a satisfying work experience from the school:

- insight into literacy development (possibly career-enhancing);
- volunteers' support to remain exclusively one-to-one;
- children required to respect volunteers' authority;
- same children supported regularly for a significant amount of time (for example 30 minutes for a specified number of weeks); this allows relationships to be built, and progress witnessed;
- volunteers never to work with their own children, and preferably not with their own children's class;
- clear instructions given for each one-to-one session;
- safeguarded debriefing time with the children's teacher;
- a predetermined working area;
- a friendly space for a break;
- a cup of tea!

Training

Ideally we would want to train *all* helpers to a point where they are able to interact appropriately in at least two of the five main stages. However, training for paid helpers may go wider, as they may well work in the school for several years.

Organized by the special needs coordinator and/or the Language/literacy postholder, possibly with outside-agency help, the training should involve all staff to some degree. At least, all need to know the content of the training programme, not only to know what extra detail their own helpers will need, but also to allay any fears about threatened professionalism.

Training for all helpers should include:

- *observation* – by observing one-to-one support at more than one stage, trainees become aware that 'Hearing reading' has many faces. From these demonstrations they see that support has to be adapted to fit the needs of different stages, and come to realize where their support fits into the overall plan;

- *instruction* – instruction needs at least two one-hour sessions, to cover:
  - the school's reading policy
  - the nature of reading
  - explanation and further demonstration of the trainees' targeted stages
  - awareness of the other stages
  - types of cues
  - the PCOS
  - the helper contract;
- *follow-up* – after working with children for about three weeks, trainees need a group follow-up session allowing them to talk through their first experiences and to ask questions. This session should be conducted by someone who was involved in the initial training;
- *probation* – there should be a few further brief occasions on which the trainees are observed working with children, after which they can discuss their work with the trainer as their 'critical friend'.

From here on, a helper will be advised by her classroom teachers, with some top-up training from time to time.

HOME–SCHOOL PARTNERSHIP

The importance of the parental role in children's reading is undeniable. Therefore the potentially powerful benefits of the parent–child bond and the opportunities for one-to-one must be linked into the school's provision, to create a good working relationship.

When the partnership is working well, the child is given a sense of security, aware that home and school share aims and values. He knows they are working together towards the same goals, and most importantly, they talk to each other!

The benefits to parents are twofold. They feel valued because the school recognizes their contribution, and are reassured by the guidance it can give them.

This home–school team, however, operates under two difficulties:

- distance – they are not under the same roof;
- numbers – quite a few relatives may work with the child, often employing different methods.

Schools must overcome these two problems in order to train the home team and to exchange observations on the child's progress.

Four routes are open to them:

- reading records,
- parents' meetings,
- personal interviews,
- written guidelines.

Reading records: teachers and parents need to speak the same language

Although home–school reading records are well established in most schools, they often become routine and repetitive. The information exchanged is frequently superficial: 'he read well', 'he tried hard'. Comments remain wide and unspecific when parents lack the technical knowledge and vocabulary to recognize identifiable signs of progress. Terms relevant to the child's developmental stage should be common currency, so that exchanges can really mean something to both parties. Moreover, these exchanges need to be regular and frequent in order to monitor the child's small steps of progress.

A reading record is working when it:

- is a regular dialogue between home and teacher;
- helps parents identify signs of progress;
- adds to the teacher's knowledge of the child;
- triggers praise at school and home for small steps of improvement.

One way to help parents recognize significant progress is to talk through a take-home set of sample comments, as a key part of a parents' meeting. Simply sending home a written explanation will not suffice.

One such set of comments (taking the child from Chiming in through to Cue talk), appears as Figure 6.3.

Figure 6.3	Signs of progress

These examples below show progress, and should be praised.

They are not in any set order.

If _____ does any one of the following, or anything similar, please write it in his/her record book.

We are interested in what your child actually says and does, so do not limit yourself to these comments. Feel free to use your own words instead of these examples:

Brought the book to us tonight
Didn't want to stop
Laughed out loud at the pictures
Guessed what was coming at the end
Wanted to talk about the pictures
A favourite book at last
Chose this book again – another favourite
Found him/her looking at the book by himself/herself
Heard him/her reciting the book, without the book
Pointed to the words as s/he recited the page
Joined in with the repetitions
Tried to read along with me

Recognized a picture as being the cover picture

Was confused by 'book language'

Told me who wrote this book and told me another one by the same author

Said '_____ is my favourite author'

Was really tired tonight so I read to him/her

Looked to see to whom the book was dedicated

Used special voices for certain characters

Asked the meaning of a word

Said 'That word's in capital letters because he's shouting'

Connected the story with his/her own life (for example 'Our gran's like that')

Got annoyed with the book because it bored him/her

Can/can't retell the story

Noticed the similarity in the pictures in two books sharing the same illustrator

Used/didn't use picture cues

Knew we couldn't start at the top of a page because it was the middle of a sentence

Knew _____ was somebody's name because s/he noticed the capital letter.

Working out

Worked out _____ by reading on, looking at the picture, and returning to it

Could give me an answer for 'How did you get that word?' for this word: _____

Told me s/he worked out **cook** by looking at the picture and recognizing **-ook**

Said the sound of the first letter/first two letters of _____ in an attempt to read it

Gave the alternative _____ for this word: _____

Gave several alternatives (i.e. _____, _____, _____) before reading this actual word on the page: _____

Said the sound of the first letter/two letters of _____ in an attempt to read it

Spotted this type of pattern: **c-ot**, and correctly built this word: _____

Spotted this type of pattern: **st-amp**, and correctly built this word: _____

Spotted this type of pattern: **sh-ar-p**, and correctly built this word: _____

_____

Kept going by himself/herself for _____ words

Kept going by himself/herself for _____ lines

Attention lasted _____ minutes

Parents' meetings

There is a great deal of information which parents need if they are to help their children to best effect, and schools have a responsibility to explain:

- the ascent-and-plateau nature of reading development;
- the timescales involved;
- what constitutes reasonable progress;
- some idea of the components of reading;
- what support is appropriate at different stages of development;
- the school's reading organization and methods;
- the range of good books;
- that learning should be stress-free and pleasurable.

There is no way all this can be imparted through written guidelines nor in a single meeting. Instead, we are talking about a gradual build-up of knowledge, through a sequence of meetings as the child progresses through the school. Any written guidance works best as a complement to these.

We have already presented some materials specifically designed for introduction at parents' meetings i.e. How to Bookbind, How to respond to Chiming in, Signs of progress, and the traffic light system; other figures from this book will also prove useful.

The way information is presented at meetings will need thought and ingenuity. We have found that information about reading can be given extra impact by creating situations where parents themselves experience reading as if they were learners. This is appreciated much more than a straight lecture. Schools may like to use the following tried-and-tested activities, adapting them to fit their own circumstances. Remember, for the messages to be effective, capitalize on the game elements, keeping it light-hearted and fun.

Activity 1 'Tear off a strip'

(Message: roles of cueing strategies, three reading levels, and tension-free support.)

This activity puts the parents into the position of reading a newspaper article at Frustration level, many of the words being quite literally unavailable, having been cut away (see Figure 6.4).

This vividly illustrates the problems of readers faced with Frustration level text. Comprehension difficulties cause visible tensions and loss of concentration. The activity forces the parents to notice how they automatically draw information from contextual cues, and how effective that strategy is. The presenter can then lead them to consider whether they encourage that same strategy in their children, or whether they inhibit them by an insistence on word-by-word accuracy.

Figure 6.4   'Tear off a strip' 1

PHONE NUMBERS TO CHANGE – AGAIN

Phone compan	ies
joined forces yester	day
in an attempt to st	ave
off the fury and ch	aos
expected to follow yet	
another num	bers
shake-up.	
They announced details o	f how
more than eight million l	and-
lines and another seven m	illion
mobile phones must chan	ge by
April 2000 ...	

Cut a strip from the right edge of a single-column article of approximately 300 words, removing no more than two words per line.
(This illustration gives only a part.)

Method
1 Give out photocopies of the cut article, now reproduced with a blank strip for writing (Figure 6.5). Give one copy per person, so that everyone can read without eye strain. Have pencils ready!
2 Ask them to work in twos or threes, one to be 'scribe'; no one should attempt the task individually.
3 Ask them to fill in the gaps at each line end.
4 Allow 3–4 minutes for this task; you will be able to judge the moment to bring it to an end, before too many people become restless.

Implications
From this point on you will be consolidating the insights you intend the parents to gain from the activity.

You will probably be asked for the author's original words, but experience has proved that it is better to give these at the end because

• if given at this point they detract from your main message, which concerns the reading process, not the text;

Figure 6.5   'Tear off a strip' 2

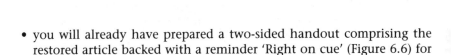

PHONE NUMBERS TO CHANGE – AGAIN

Phone compan
joined forces yester
in an attempt to st
off the fury and ch
expected to follow yet
another num
shake-up.
They announced details o
more than eight million l
lines and another seven m
mobile phones must chan
April 2000 ...

- you will already have prepared a two-sided handout comprising the restored article backed with a reminder 'Right on cue' (Figure 6.6) for distribution at the end of the meeting.

1 Point out that the restored passage would probably take only one minute to read! If they had persisted to the bitter end on this deleted passage it may well have taken up to 20 minutes.

  Although the passage has lost approximately 20 per cent of its words, the consequent loss of comprehension is closer to 50 per cent. Explain that the reason for this activity is to put them in a similar situation to one often experienced by a child, and that actually comprehension loss for a child occurs with even greater rapidity. With only 10 per cent of the words unread, children lose anything from 50 per cent to as much as 80 per cent of the meaning.

2 Introduce the term 'Frustration level', with its definition (see page 71).

3 Point out that they automatically resorted to their normal fluent reading strategies:
  - reading on past the problem
  - back-tracking
  - using strings of letters to prompt or clinch suggested words
  - keeping up a swift pace, not plodding word by word
  - estimating possibilities
  - refining original suggestions

- using their prior knowledge of the subject matter, and of what news-papers sound like
- coming to decisions by talking together.
  These strategies are listed on the reminder (Figure 6.6), for later distribution.

4 Warn of the dangers of Frustration level.
- How would they like it if most of their own reading was as hard work as this newspaper article? When children are put on books at Frustration level they soon show signs of fatigue, resentment, demotivation, loss of concentration.
- Point out that Frustration level is reached from a smaller word-loss than one might suppose i.e. 10 per cent. So, do not push a child onto the next level of a scheme if it is his Frustration level.
- Suggest that they learn to run a quick check on a child's book for how many possibly difficult words there are in every hundred. Beware the recent birthday present whose back cover announces it as 'suitable for 7- to 8-year-olds'. That may be appropriate for the interest level; the reading level could well be much higher. Frustration level books should be read *to* children.

5 Sum up the lessons to be learned from this newspaper activity:
- Children should be prompted and encouraged to use the same strategies they used, listed for them to take home.
- There is value in working with someone to puzzle out meanings. Compare such friendly sharing with tension-filled waiting, almost like putting a child in the big black Mastermind chair!

Figure 6.6	**Right on cue**

We kept on reading, past any problems.
We then back-tracked to take a new run at problems.
We kept up a good pace. We did not plod, word by word.
We tried out a variety of possibilities for unknown words.
We checked possibilities against:

- what we already knew about the subject;
- meaning;
- grammar;
- word length;
- any given letters.

We let the first few letters of some words trigger possibilities.
We came to decisions by talking together.
Some words came to us from saying – not reading – the surrounding sentence(s) over and over again.

This is the way my child needs to work. I promise to help him.

Activity 2 'The Generation Game'

(Message: whatever your age, you read at three different levels.)

This activity is intended to convey the concept that everyone operates at three different reading levels at every stage in life. It illustrates the idea that the levels describe performance, not text. Any single text could be labelled differently for three different people, depending on their varying experiences of reading, work and life. The activity helps parents to understand why and how their child should experience all three levels regularly.

Method
1 Give each person a Bicycle chart (Figure 4.14), showing the three reading levels, explaining what they mean.
2 Show an OHT of a list (Figure 6.7) of everyday reading matter, selected to be as unthreatening as possible. (For example, naming *any* fiction could be threatening to somebody!)
    Each item is numbered, to lessen the writing task facing the audience.
3 Ask them to work on their own, reassuring them that no one will want to see their answers. Invite them to decide in which column each item belongs, for them. They need write only each item's number.
4 Allow some 2–3 minutes for this task. Once again, you will be able to judge when to move on.

Figure 6.7	'The Generation Game' 1

1 tax form
2 holiday insurance policy
3 free newspaper
4 instructions on building DIY furniture
5 'You have definitely won £60,000 . . . (provided that . . .)'
6 opening offer from new restaurant
7 helping with child's textbook for homework
8 computer manual
9 knitting pattern
10 car manual
11 letter from a friend

Implications
Elaborate the concepts to be gained from the activity:

1 Show the OHT of your own classification of these items (Figure 6.8) as a focus for generalized commentary.
    Comment that everyone has three levels throughout life, but as experience grows, reading matter may shift from one category to another. For example, a car manual might move from Frustration to

Figure 6.8	'The Generation Game' 2	

Frustration	**Instructional**	**Independent**
1 tax form	2 holiday insurance policy	3 free newspaper
4 instructions on building DIY furniture	9 knitting pattern	11 letter from a friend
8 computer manual	5 'You have definitely won £60,000 (provided that . . .)'	6 opening offer from new restaurant
10 car manual	7 helping with child's textbook for homework	

Independent on buying your first car. Also different people will classify the same item (for example a knitting pattern) differently.

Point out that there could be other possible classifications; for example, for a computer programmer the computer manual would not be in the Frustration category.

2 Relate their activity to their children's reading.

Without requiring public answers, ask them to consider:

– whether they have recently inadvertently asked their child to read at Frustration level.

– whether they have ever thought, or even said, that their child was not being sufficiently challenged when reading at Independent level.

(This 'Generation Game' makes a useful introduction to the traffic light system)

Activity 3 'Des. res.'

(Message: explanation of 'cue', and the range of cues on offer.)

This activity puts parents into a situation in which the reading process is forcibly slowed down, to a point at which the cues can be observed. Through listing them, they come to realize that fluent readers use a variety of cues, and are helped to appreciate the valuable contribution of each one.

Method

1 Ask your audience to have a go at reading an estate agent's advertisement – with a difference. It is written in mirror-writing, and upside down (Figure 6.9).

2 Give out one copy per person. Ask them to work in twos or threes, not alone. Warn against cheating: severe penalties will be imposed on anyone found to be holding the paper up to the light – no coffee at the coffee break!

Figure 6.9   'Des. res.'

> Desirable semi-detached residence with
> all mod. cons, 2 recep. + bed., bathrm,
> utility, verandah. In need of some
> modernisation. Easily managed garden.
> Very close to useful amenities. All reasonable
> offers considered.

3 Allow 2–4 minutes. It is useful to circulate, listening for the strategies being used. You will be able to judge when to bring it to an end.
4 Show an OHT of the reversed passage. Read it slowly, encouraging contributions from your audience. Draw from them what 'clues' they used. Weave in any comments overheard earlier, without naming individuals, of course.
5 Show an OHT of types of 'clues' (Figure 6.10). Point out that you began by using the term 'clue', but now are changing it to the technical term 'cue'. This is the term used in the National Curriculum, and in school.

Figure 6.10   **Types of 'clues' used to read the estate agent's advertisement**

Sight vocabulary
Letter knowledge
Using context
Using experience to work out words
Reading 'Between the lines'

Implications
Summarize the points which you hope the parents will have gained from this activity:

1 Show a prepared OHT of comments from previous groups (Figure 6.11): 'Here's one I made earlier . . .!' Allow time for comment, and bring out the following points:
   – all groups used a balance of cues – the activity showed it is not possible to stick with one type of cue
   – groups got started via different cues.

2 Put the questions (without requiring answers):
  - Are they now aware of strategies which they themselves use automatically?
  - Have they been allowing their child to use them?
  - Will they do so in the future?

For taking home
'Right on cue', (Figure 6.6) linked to Activity 1 (page 163), makes an equally useful reminder here.

Figure 6.11	Types of cues used in 'Des. res.'

Examples of comments revealing cues used to read the estate agent's advertisement

Sight vocabulary

'Let's see if we can spot any word . . .'

Letter knowledge

'Oh! They're **as**!'
'You need to know letter shapes . . . these **as** look so like **ys**'
'We worked all the letters out'
'We got the first letter and then the word just came'

Using context

'Once you're into the swing of each little passage you don't need the
   letters'
'You get that 'cos you know the phrase'
'We just went through all the words and "amenities" came out'
'We didn't go all through "modernization", all we got was **mod**'
'Knowing the pattern . . . you get a sense of the pattern'

Using experience to work out words

'**Bathroom** was hard because the vowels were missing, but we knew what
   was usually next to the bedroom'
'I used to live in India, so I'm used to houses with verandahs'
'My husband's an estate agent . . . I speak the language!'

Reading Between the lines

'We all know what "in need of some modernization" means!'
'"all reasonable offers" – Ha! They're desperate!'

Publicity for parents' meetings

The national press may tell us of a wide interest among parents in reading standards, yet quite often evening meetings have to be well advertised if they are to succeed, and every school will recognize that it can be difficult to attract those parents it most needs to meet. The importance of these meetings should be reflected in the methods used to publicize them, and the following suggestions are known to be helpful:

- A personally addressed letter is more effective than a couple of lines in a routine bulletin.
- A newsletter reference may support letters, but it never replaces them.
- Personal invitations written by children to their own parents are powerful reminders.
- Letters need the backing of posters in prominent positions around the school.
- One school gave out new books and bright new plastic reading wallets, but *only* on meeting the parents face to face. (Children at this school were dragging in their parents by the hand!)

Letters home

All letters should be as carefully thought out as the meetings themselves. They are a key approach (along with the 'word at the gate') to attract not only the enthusiastic parent, but also those who are reluctant, even fearful.

The pre-school invitation must establish that the school sees parents as important and is keen to work in partnership, while reassuring parents that they will get a friendly reception.

Figure 6.12 is a sample format for one invitation letter, the principles of which are equally applicable to invitations to all meetings.

Following any session on reading, those parents who have been unable to attend should be contacted by a second letter, giving them a further opportunity.

Repeat sessions may seem an overwhelming undertaking, but they need not be delivered by the same members of staff, and there may even be help available from local education authority support services.

Personal interviews

There are parents who do not attend school meetings, and this is not necessarily due to apathy or hostility. There may be genuine problems in leaving the house, or significant unease about coming into contact with the school and all it represents. However, they may well be the people the teacher most needs to see, and perhaps even just one home visit, or individual meeting in school, could be instrumental in breaking a cycle of perpetuating problems.

This is easier said than done, but where it is achieved, it is through one or more of these arrangements:

Figure 6.12   **Sample invitation to a parents' meeting**

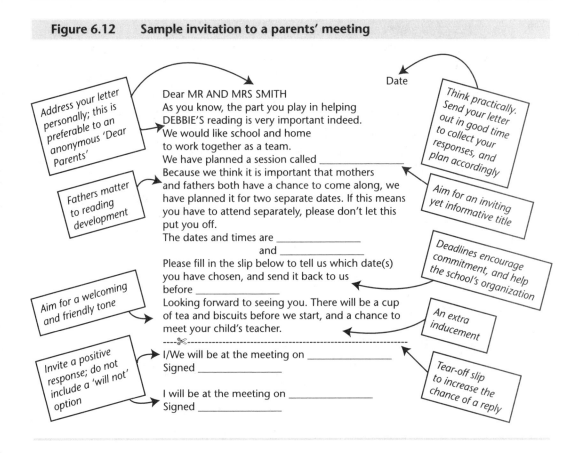

- finding a member of staff willing and able to undertake this type of work (which may or may not include the head, deputy or special needs coordinator);
- ensuring that teacher has cover so it can be done in school time;
- involving one of the support agencies (social worker, learning support service, community liaison officer, etc.).

The meetings must be with the parents' consent, arranged by telephone, by catching them at the gate, by a personal letter which asks directly for the opportunity to talk, or by working through an agency which already has personal contact. Cold-calling is not an option.

When these get-togethers are in school, try to have a pleasant room set aside, which feels more like a home and less like a school room.

A practical demonstration of reading support, usually with the parents' own child, will accomplish far more than discussion alone. It is often rewarded by parental remarks such as 'I see what you mean now!' or 'I've not been doing it like that . . . I've never let him read on past the hard word . . .' or 'Oh! I've been splitting the words up letter by letter.' The outcome can often be a considerable turnround in practice, maybe changing a strongly held misconception about how to teach reading, to something more closely aligned to the school's method. To other parents it can offer clarification, perhaps reassuring them that they are actually on the right lines but that things may just take a little longer. To yet others it might highlight small steps of progress of which they had been unaware.

Finally, even parents whose own reading skills are poor can have their self-esteem raised by being convinced of the value their positive support will bring. This can be as straightforward as making sure that there *is* a reading time-slot at home.

Written guidelines

After any explanatory time with parents, whether in a meeting or in an individual interview, the school should be able to offer them printed guidelines to take away as a reminder and a reference.

Various items in this book lend themselves to this purpose. For instance:

- How to Bookbind,
- How to respond to Chiming in,
- Signs of progress,
- The traffic light system.

Ideally, written materials should never replace meetings.

CONCLUSION

So here we are at the end of a chapter which has made the case for the team approach and has demonstrated some ways in which it can be initiated.

In very many children's lives a team is there quite naturally, with, on the one hand, parents and extended family available and eager to play their parts, and on the other the school with its professional and non-professional personnel. Moreover, even for those children who lack strong home input there is still usually some team support within the school.

Without his team, Sam's 'readingful' day as described in Chapter 4 would not have been filled with such a variety of reading experiences. Through them he enjoyed the advantages of two contrasting styles of teaching. He and the rest of the class benefited from the planned word study that his teacher linked to their work on the Beaufort Scale, with her careful direct presentation of the sounds of **ch** in **chart**, **school** and **machine** – an appropriately didactic session. They learned similarly from having their attention drawn to the way in which authors' different purposes produce different registers, as they were led to compare scientific and poetic texts. Conversely, Sam also benefited while in a one-to-one situation from the skilful supporting questions of his helper, as he tackled a difficult word (**soared**), in a book which was of his own choosing.

In this personalized and interactive session, he moved between meaning and mechanics, employing contextual and letter clues to add a word to his vocabulary and to memorize a phoneme–grapheme bond (. . . **oar**). These two complementary teaching styles contributed equally to his reading development. Sam also experienced reinforcement and consolidation from the other members of his team that day. Every member contributed differently, yet importantly.

Let us conclude now by returning to the model with which we began: reading as having three permanent components, with the reader needing to surf between them to take and make meaning. This accomplishment stems from a dauntingly wide span of learning, some of which will have to be promoted by the transmission of information, some of which will have to be developed as an active, constructive, essentially individual process. Such a complex task clearly demands the team approach if the goal of effective tuition in the whole range of reading skills is to be attained.

References

Adams, M.J. (1990) *Beginning To Read*. Cambridge, MA: MIT Press.

Adams, M.J. (1991) Beginning to read: a critique by literacy professionals and a response by Marilyn Jager Adams, *The Reading Teacher*, 44(6) February: 371.

Ayto, J. (1990) *Dictionary of Word Origins*. London: Bloomsbury.

Beal, G. (1991) *Book of Words*. London: Kingfisher.

Betts, E.A. (1957) *Foundations of Reading Instruction*. New York: American Book Company, cited in Ruth Strang (1972) Informal reading inventories, in A. Melnik and J. Merritt (eds) *The Reading Curriculum*. London: University of London Press.

Bradley, L. (1990) Rhyming connections in learning to read and spell, in P.D. Pumfrey and C.D. Elliott (eds) *Children's Difficulties in Reading, Spelling and Writing*. Basingstoke: Falmer Press.

Bryant, P. and Bradley, L. (1985) *Children's Reading Problems*. Oxford: Blackwell.

Chall, J. (1983) *Stages of Reading Development*. New York: McGraw Hill.

Clymer, T. (1972) What is reading?, in A. Melnik and J. Merritt (eds) *Reading, Today and Tomorrow*. London: University of London Press.

Cox, B. (chair) (1989) *Report of National Curriculum Working Group for English: English for Ages 5–16*. London: DES.

Davies, A. and Ritchie, D. (1998) *THRASS: Teaching Handwriting, Reading and Spelling Skills*. Chester: THRASS, UK.

Department for Education and Employment [DfEE] (1995) *English in the National Curriculum*. London: DfEE.

DfEE (1998) *National Literacy Strategy Framework for Teaching*. London: DfEE.

Fry, E. (1968) A readability formula that saves time, *Journal of Reading*, 11: 513–16, 575–8.

Gattegno, G. (1962) *Words in Colour*. London: Educational Explorers.

Goodman, K. (1976a) Behind the eye: what happens in reading, in H. Singer and R.B. Ruddell (eds) *Theoretical Models and Processes of Reading*. Newark, DE: Lawrence Erlbaum Associates and IRA.

Goodman, K. (1976b) Unity in reading, in H. Singer and R.B. Ruddell (eds) *Theoretical Models and Processes of Reading*. Newark, DE: Lawrence Erlbaum Associates and IRA, pp. 833–9.

Gray, W.S. (1960) The major aspects of reading, in H.M. Robinson (ed.) *Sequential Development of Reading Abilities*. Supplementary Educational Monograph no. 90, University of Chicago Press, pp. 8–24.

Harrison, C. (1996) *What Teachers Need to Know about Reading*. Shepreth: UKRA.

Huey, E.B. (1908) *The Psychology and Pedagogy of Reading*. New York: Macmillan; reprinted 1973, Cambridge, MA: MIT Press.

Hunt, R., Page, T. and Pemberton, S. (1985) Teachers' manual to *The Oxford Reading Tree*. Oxford: Oxford University Press.

Kingman, Sir J. (chair) (1988) *Report of Committee of Inquiry into the Teaching of English Language*. London: HMSO.

Manguel, A. (1997) *The History of Reading*. London: Harper Collins.

Peters, M. and Smith, B. (1993) *Spelling in Context*. Windsor: NFER-Nelson.

Ramsden, M. (1993) *Rescuing Spelling*. Crediton: Southgate Publishing.

Strang, R. (1972) The nature of reading, in A. Melnik and J. Merrit (eds) *Reading: Today and Tomorrow*. London: University of London Press.

Wells, G. (1986) *The Meaning Makers*. London: Hodder and Stoughton.

Wray, D. (1995) Comprehension monitoring, metacognition, and other mysterious processes in C. Gains and D. Wray (eds) *Reading: Issues and Directions*. Stafford: NASEN, summarizing Vygotsky (1978) *Mind in Society*. Cambridge, MA: Harvard University Press.

Related reading

Introduction and Rationale

Hearing reading

Campbell, Robin (1981) An approach to analysing teachers' verbal moves in hearing children read, *Journal of Research in Reading*, 4(1): 43–56.

Hale, Angela (1980) The social relationships implicit in approaches to hearing reading, *Reading*, 14(2): 24–30.

NATE (1984) *Children Reading to Their Teachers*. Sheffield: NATE.

Plant, Richard (1986) Reading research: its influence on classroom practice, *Educational Research*, 28(2): 126–31.

Southgate, V., Arnold, H. and Johnson, S. (1981) *Extending Beginning Reading*. London: Heinemann Educational Books for the Schools Council.

Stierer, Barry (1983) A researcher reading teachers reading children reading, in Margaret Meek (ed.) *Opening Moves*, Bedford Way Papers no. 17. London: Institute of Education.

Cues

Harrison, Colin (1996) *What Teachers Need to Know about Reading*. Shepreth: UKRA. Section Two reviews the current evaluation of Goodman's ideas.

Littlefair, Alison (1991) *Reading All Types of Writing*. Buckingham: Open University Press.
  For an account of genre and register.

Littlefair, Alison (1992) *Genres in the Classroom*. Shepreth: UKRA Minibook 1.

Smith, Frank (1978) *Reading*. Cambridge: Cambridge University Press, p. 13.
  A discussion of visual and non-visual information, and the trading which takes place between them.

Snowling, M. and Nation, K. (1997) Language, phonology and learning to read, in C. Hulme and M. Snowling (eds) *Dyslexia: Biology, Cognition, and Intervention*. London: Whurr, p. 162.

This paper notes certain findings which 'underline the fact that there is more to reading than decoding'.

Stanovich, K. (1980) Towards an interactive-compensatory model of individual differences in the development of reading fluency, *Reading Research Quarterly*, 16: 32–71.

This paper refers to evidence that top-down and bottom-up processing are not necessarily sequential.

Chapter 1 Bookbinding

Story

Rosen, Harold (1984) Narratology and the teacher, in H. Rosen (ed.) *Stories and Meanings*. Sheffield: NATE.

Wells, Gordon (1986) *The Meaning Makers*. London: Hodder and Stoughton, Chapter 10.

Broad cues

Dombey, Henrietta (1983) Learning the language of books, in Margaret Meek (ed.) *Opening Moves*, Bedford Way Papers no. 17. London: Institute of Education.

Fox, Carol (1983) Talking like a book, in Margaret Meek (ed.) *Opening Moves*, Bedford Way Papers no. 17. London: Institute of Education.

Meek, Margaret (1988) *How Texts Teach What Readers Learn*. Stroud, Glos.: Thimble Press.

Reading with real purpose

Breen, Michael (1983) Authenticity in the language classroom, *Applied Linguistics*, 6(1): 60–70.

Reading the pictures

Bennett, Jill (1979) *Learning to Read With Picture Books*. Stroud, Glos.: Thimble Press.

Graham, Judith (1990) *Pictures on the Page*. Sheffield: NATE.

Meek, Margaret (1988) *How Texts Teach What Readers Learn*. Stroud, Glos.: Thimble Press.

Sight vocabulary

Frith, Uta (1985) Beneath the surface of developmental dyslexia, in K.E. Patterson, J.C. Marshall and M. Coltheart (eds) *Surface Dyslexia*. Hillsdale, NY: Lawrence Erlbaum.

This paper includes a model of reading development showing the early place of sight vocabulary, as the logographic stage.

Gough, P.B., Ehri, L.C. and Trieman, R. (eds) (1992) *Reading Acquisition*. London: Lawrence Erlbaum Associates.

Phonological awareness

Bryant, Peter and Bradley, Lynette (1985) *Children's Reading Problems*. Oxford: Blackwell.

Goswami, Usha (1997) Learning to read in different orthographies, in C. Hulme and M. Snowling (eds) *Dyslexia: Biology, Cognition, and Intervention*. London: Whurr.

Goswami, Usha and Bryant, Peter (1990) *Phonological Skills and Learning to Read*. Hillsdale, NY: Lawrence Erlbaum Associates.

James, Frances (1996) *Phonological Awareness: Classroom Strategies*, UKRA Minibook 7. Shepreth: UKRA.

Hynds, Jeff (1997) *Children's Books Providing Basic Experience of the English Spelling System: A Bibliography*. Biggin Hill: Jeff Hynds Books.

Reading as meaning-making

Barthes, Roland (1975) *S/Z*. London: Jonathan Cape.
  '. . . the reader is no longer a consumer but a producer of text'
Genette, J. (1980) *Narrative Discourse*. Oxford: Basil Blackwell.
  '. . . the real author of the narrative is not only he who tells it, but at times even more he who hears it'
Iser, W. (1978) *The Act of Reading*. London: Routledge and Kegan Paul.
Meek, Margaret (1982) *Learning to Read*. London: Bodley Head.
  'Some successful readers say that they feel they are helping to create the work *with* the author' (her italics)

Chapter 2 Chiming in

Waterland, Liz (1985) *Read With Me*. Stroud, Glos.: Thimble Press.

Chapter 3 Cue talk

Donaldson, Margaret (1978) *Children's Minds*. London: Fontana Collins.
Harrison, Colin (1996) *What Teachers Need to Know about Reading*. Shepreth: UKRA, pp. 27–8.
  Notes the widespread use by teachers of that expression 'it just clicks': 'The reader's ability to analyse and articulate what he is doing (metacognition)'
Vygotsky, L. (1962) *Thought and Language*. Cambridge, MA: MIT Press.
Wray, David (1994) *Literacy and Awareness*. London: Hodder and Stoughton.

Chapter 4 Assisted reading

Knowledge about reading

NATE (1988) Submission to the Committee of Inquiry into the Teaching of English Language (chair Sir J. Kingman), in M. Jones and A. West (eds) *Learning Me Your Language*. London: Mary Glasgow Publications.
  The place of explicit knowledge in language learning

Ten supportive actions

Share, David (1995) Phonological re-coding and self-teaching: the sine qua non of reading acquisition, *Cognition*, 55: 151–218.

Automaticity in recognizing phonic elements at speed

Adams, Marilyn Jager (1990) *Beginning to Read*. Cambridge, MA: MIT Press.

Chapter 5 Branching out

Self-teaching

Stanovich, K.E. (1986) Matthew effects in reading: some consequences of individual differences in the acquisition of literacy, *Reading Research Quarterly*,
21(4): 360–407.

Paired reading

Hewison, J. and Tizard, J. (1980) Parental involvement and reading attainment,
British Journal of Educational Psychology, 50: 209–15.
Topping, K. (1986) WHICH parental involvement in reading scheme? *Reading*,
20(3): 148–56.
Topping, K. and Wolfendale, S. (1985) *Parental Involvement in Children's Reading*.
London: Croom Helm.

Reading journals

Hackman, Susan (1986) Reading journals, *Reading*, 20(3): 197–201.

Register break puzzles

Littlefair, Alison (1991) *Reading All Types of Writing*. Buckingham: Open
University Press.

Three-speed reading

Pugh, A.K. (1978) *Silent Reading: An Introduction to its Study and Teaching*. London:
Heinemann Educational Books.

DARTs

Clymer, T. (1972) What is reading, in A. Melnik and J. Merritt (eds) *Reading Today
and Tomorrow*. London: University of London Press, pp. 56–60 (The Barrett
Taxonomy of levels of questioning).
Davies, F. and Greene, T. (1984) *Reading for Learning in the Sciences*. Edinburgh:
Oliver and Boyd.
Lunzer, E. and Gardner, K. (1984) *Learning from the Written Word*. Edinburgh:
Oliver and Boyd.
Morris, A. and Stewart-Dore, N. (1984) *Learning to Learn from Text*. North Ryde,
New South Wales: Addison Wesley.
Wray, D. and Lewis, M. (1994) *The Exeter Extending Literacy Project (EXEL)*. Exeter:
Exeter School of Education.

Creative follow-ups

Benton, M. and Fox, G. (1985) *Teaching Literature 9–14*. Oxford: Oxford University
Press.

Chapter 6 The team approach

Moyles, Janet (1997) *Jills of All Trades? ...: Classroom Assistants in KS1 Classes.* Leicester: University of Leicester School of Education and the Association of Teachers and Lecturers.

Hutchings, M. (1997) The impact of a specialist teacher assistant training programme on the development of classroom assistants, *Early Years*, 18(1): 35–9.

Toomey, D. (1993) Parents hearing their children read: a review. Rethinking the lessons of the Haringey Project, *Educational Research*, 35(3): 223–36.

Wolfendale, Sheila (1992) *Empowering Parents and Teachers – Working for Children.* London: Cassell.

Wolfendale, Sheila and Topping, Keith (eds) (1996) *Family Involvement in Literacy – Effective Partnerships in Education.* London: Cassell.

Index

Page numbers in bold indicate the main entry on a particular subject